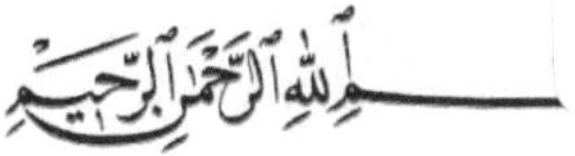

A Breeze from the East

Poems in Mashriqi English

by

Wael Almahdi

Crescent Books

Crescent Books

Prepared and Typeset
by Erzen Pashaj.

Paperback
ISBN:
978-1-954935-12-9

Subjects:
Poetry | Ghazal | Islam
Rumi | Language

First edition
Text copy edited by Stella Williams.
Cover image: "Farhad Carves a Milk Channel for Shirin,"
Folio 74, Khamsa (Quintet) by Nizami of Ganja (16th Century).
Cover design by Wael Almahdi & Stella Williams.
Printed in the United States of America

"A Breeze from the East is a remarkable collection of poems that captures the essence of human experience with depth and grace. Almahdi masterfully weaves the familiar with the unexpected, blending the sacred and the whimsical. Each poem invites reflection and emotion, leaving you both amazed and deeply moved. Whether you are a seasoned lover of poetry or new to the genre, this collection is a journey worth taking— one that lingers long after the final page."

—**Laureta Rexha,** author of *When My Absence Becomes a Moon*

Dedication

To my parents, wife, kids, and siblings,
who have always supported me.
And to those learners who enjoy
the compulsion of finding order
and truth in words, also known
by society as "nerds."

Fazl u hunar zāyi' ast tā nanumāyand;
Ūd bar ātash nahand u mushk bisāyand.

Art and virtue are in vain unless they be displayed;
As musk is ground and agarwood is on the flames arrayed.

—Sa'di

Contents

کؤنتَّنتس

Foreword

This collection is both rare and stunning, a true gem in the world of poetry. As you read, you're compelled to slow down, experiencing the deliberate pauses and the search for elusive words in languages you may not fully master. Wael Almahdi's intricate play with words, languages, and concepts is nothing short of extraordinary. This is not just poetry; it's an opus of a poet who captivates us with both subtlety and grandeur, leaving an indelible impression.

As I journeyed through Wael's poems, I found myself drawn into a dance of meanings, where each line held the weight of a thousand unspoken thoughts. His ability to weave together the familiar and the unfamiliar, the simple and the profound, reminded me of the delicate balance all poets strive for, yet few achieve. There were moments when I had to pause, not just to understand the words, but to feel them—really feel them—in the way only Wael's unique voice can evoke.

Reflecting on his work, I am filled with both awe and a wry smile, knowing that Wael manages to say with ease what the rest of us labor to express. His poetry dances between the sacred and the playful, leaving you marveling at his skill while also chuckling at the sheer audacity of his craft.

Wael doesn't just write poetry—he invites you into a world where every word is carefully chosen, each silence is weighty, and every emotion is felt deeply. It's a world of words that, once entered, you'll not want to leave.

Flamur Vehapi, author of *Verses of the Heart*

Introduction

Mashriqi English: A Novel Poetic Register

This collection is written in Mashriqi English, a poetic register rooted in Modern English grammar and vocabulary and enriched by the lexical, esthetic, and thematic resources of the Arabic and Persian poetic traditions. This register strives not only to incorporate linguistic elements common to these two traditions but also evokes the cultural and historical textures associated with them. The adjective *mashriqī* is derived from *Mashriq*, which in modern Arabic usage is understood as *the East* in its wider geographical, civilizational, and cultural senses (*Mashriq* is also found in Persian and Urdu with some overlap in usage. Thus the eminent Urdu poet Muhammad Iqbal is called *Shāʿir-i Mashriq*, "The Poet of the East"). Starting in the 7th century CE, a new, post-Islamic, stage of the Persian language was heavily influenced by Arabic vocabulary, poetic form, and themes. This partly creolized vernacular, with its simple grammar, flexible syntax, and readiness for lexical borrowing, furnished a fertile soil for a world-renowned poetic tradition that spans fourteen centuries. It has in turn influenced other Islamicate languages, which in time produced noteworthy literary traditions of their own. By aligning itself with this Arabic-influenced Persianate tradition and its descendants, Mashriqi English seeks to emulate such notable historical precedents as Urdu, Chagatai, and Ottoman Turkish. These languages constitute a historical, cultural, and–dare we say spiritual–grouping in which remarkable commonalities of worldview and sentiment are expressed in almost identical vocabulary, offering the poet a consistent but malleable wellspring of artistic inspiration and reinterpretation, in the original languages themselves and in the poetic register I have termed Mashriqi English.

Despite its expansive presence in public spaces, the media, and daily conversation, this shared Perso-Arabic (thus termed because Arabic influence–particularly on vocabulary and script–on Indic and Turkic languages was not direct but mediated through Persian) heritage remains under-studied and only implicitly, informally recognized. In a vast region stretching from Nouakchott to Ürümqi to Jakarta, one can observe common concepts expressed in nearly identical terms in public spaces and in everyday speech. These words, often signposts for deeper meta-cultural layers of sense and usage, are not only prominent in influential written works, but have also been imprinted on the speech and thinking of the average speaker.

Mashriqi English is not a distinct language, nor is it a creole, nor an artificial language. Far from being a "watered-down" version of English, it employs the full armamentarium of contemporary Modern English vocabulary, idiom, grammar, and phonology. English is uniquely susceptible to this literary reinterpretation as it is a versatile and expressive vehicle at the forefront of global shifts in culture, technology, and worldview. Into this flexible substrate the poet seeks to consciously and tastefully incorporate Perso-Arabic elements, all the while maintaining a keen historical sense and a respect for correct usage. This deliberate and discerning attitude reflects itself in the emblematic Perso-Arabic terms introduced into Mashriqi English, as well as specific poetic forms, such as the muwasshaḥ, ghazal, and rubāʿiyah, possibly even extending to Perso-Arabic ʿarūḍ, the classical prosody system that governs poetic meter in Arabic and Persian. In this collection, however, the customary accentual-syllabic English meters have been adhered to.

The result, I hope, will be poetry that reflects the intricacies and spirit of the Islamicate imaginary, already distilled in the hermetic vessel of languages such as Arabic, Persian, Urdu, Chagatai, Ottoman Turkish, Punjabi, Malay, Swahili, and many others. To sketch this parent stem and its diverse flowerings, I will present and briefly explain passages from Uzbek, Urdu, and Persian with Perso-Arabic words underlined.

Uzbek

اولار عقل و وجدان صاحبی دیلار وبیر بیرلا ایکا برادرلرجا معامله قیلیشلاری ضرور

Ular aql va vijdon sohibidilar va bir-birla iga birodarlarcha muomala qilishlari zarur.

(They are endowed with reason and conscience and should act towards one another in a spirit of brotherhood.)

In this second sentence from the first clause of The Universal Declaration of Human Rights, we find that the words for "mind," "conscience," "possessor," "treatment," and "necessary" are Perso-Arabic borrowings. This pattern is also typical of Urdu, Turkish, and other culturally related languages, where many abstract and high-register terms are borrowed from Persian or Arabic through Persian. For example, *aql*, "reason, mind," has spread almost unmodified to all the languages that belong to the Perso-Arabic tradition. Similarly, *birodar*, the Persian word for "brother" or "comrade," is known in Turkish, Urdu, and others. Although the English "spirit" is not rendered literally here, the Uzbek equivalent *ruh* is a Perso-Arabic borrowing.

Vijdon, from Arabic *wijdān*, "inner world," gained the sense "conscience" in Persian and was subsequently borrowed by multiple languages, including Turkish (*vicdan*). It derives from a fecund Arabic root which produces, among others, words like *mawjūd*, "present, existent," and *wujūd*, "existence." The latter forms part of a potent set of Sufi terms (including *waḥdat al-wujūd*, the concept that all existence ultimately emanates from and merges into the Divine essence). Mashriqi English is envisioned as inheriting this contiguous tapestry of associations, both mundane and sacred, which remains remarkably consistent across tens of living languages.

Urdu

بسکہ دشوار ہے ہر کام کا آساں ہونا

آدمی کو بھی میسر نہیں انساں ہونا

Bas ke dushwār hai har kām kā āsāñ honā
Adāmī ko bhī muyassar nahīñ insān honā

(It's very difficult to make every task easy
But it's impossible for every person to become human.)

Urdu is a prime example of a literary language heavily influenced by the Perso-Arabic tradition. The above verse by the eminent Urdu poet Mirzā Ghālib is etched on the psyches of millions of people across South Asia. It showcases several common Perso-Arabic borrowings, words that have been integral to the vocabulary of Urdu and other culturally related languages for centuries. The Persian *bas* ("enough, too much") is known in South Asia, the Arabic-speaking world, and East Africa, while *har* ("every, each") is also found in Turkish, Uzbek, Azerbaijani, Turkmen, and a host of other Turkic languages. A particularly emblematic Arabic word, *insān*, "human being," is part of the discourse and phonology of at least a billion people.[1] In fact, this word is so fundamental to Turkish vocabulary that, during the 1928–1932 language reform—which aimed to replace Perso-Arabic vocabulary with native Turkic terms—no suitable alternative could be found. The reform was only

---

[1] According to a very rough estimate based on my own research.

partially successful, and *insan*, along with thousands of other Perso-Arabic words, remains a vital part of the Turkish lexicon today. When speakers of languages within the Perso-Arabic *Sprachbund* encounter *insān* in Mashriqi English, it will convey a coherent set of familiar concepts and connotations.

Persian

بشـنو اين نی چون شـكايت ميكند

از جدايي ها حكايت ميكند

Beshno īn nay chūn <u>shikāyat</u> mekunad
Az judāīhā <u>ḥikāyat</u> mekunad

(Listen to the reed's <u>lament</u>—and how it tells a <u>tale</u> of separation)

This is the iconic first verse of the *Masnawī-yi Ma'nawī* by the world-renowned Sufi master and poet Jalaluddin Rumi. It is impossible to quantify the influence of this monumental poem on the Persianate and wider Islamicate world. The emblematic *nay*, "reed" (*ney* in Modern Western Persian and *nāy* in Arabic) symbolizes the separated human soul and its longing for reunion with the divine. The soul's lament is rendered with Arabic *shikāyat*, while the narrative of the soul's arduous journey is described with the rhyming Arabic *ḥikāyat*. Persian has not only adopted thousands of Arabic words, but has also completely naturalized them as part of its own vocabulary, both in writing and speech. Subsequently, this already cohesive and enriching usage was adopted by languages within the Persianate cultural sphere like Urdu and the Turkic languages. In this collection, I have translated the first few verses of the *Masnawī* into Mashriqi English.

Why Mashriqi English?

It would be lazy, but not entirely disingenuous, to claim that artistic beauty–whether visual or literary–requires no justification on the part of its originator. This is true for poetry, with its beauty-centered polarities of tradition and freshness, and especially true for Arabic and Persianate verse, which for centuries has reshaped its foundational *prima materia* into ever new and wondrous pieces of art. In Mashriqi English, I hope that this archetypal material will fuse with a modern English sensibility to produce an idiom at once familiar and fresh. Still, if one is to attempt the seemingly unprecedented literary endeavor of consciously adorning one language with the organically woven attire of a culturally and historically distinct group of languages, one must at least attempt such a justification.

First, as we have seen, the effects of Arabic and Persian influence on other languages are often visibly and audibly evident, yet rarely explored in any formal sense. Global English–versatile and flexible, with its uninflected adjectives, verbalizable nouns, minimally declined verbs, and openness to borrowing–is the ideal substrate on which to graft the scion of this shared oral culture. English vocabulary and turns of phrase has already been immeasurably enriched by layers of Norman French, Latin, and Greek, so a further Perso-Arabic stratum would only deepen its already well-formed expressive potential.

Moreover, it would not be a stretch to claim that English is the *de facto* language of international Islamicate culture and discourse–whether online or in real life venues such as conferences and universities. This is hardly surprising: many Muslim-majority countries have inherited English as a secondary language from former colonizers, while others have no choice but to use it to convey their message to a global audience–just as the authors of the Christian Gospels chose *koiné* Greek, the international medium of their time. In such an environment, Mashriqi English would already be partly familiar to countless individuals who have spent years learning and using English.

Second, Mashriq English can serve as a bridge to poetry within the Perso-Arabic tradition for those without the knowledge or resources to engage directly with the original languages. This holds true of both English speakers whose heritage includes a Perso-Arabic-influenced language and those who simply seek a deeper sense of the movement of image and sentiment in those traditions. Naturally, Mashriqi English is no substitute for the direct understanding and enjoyment of the source languages' poetic and cultural wealth. Yet the hope is that it might be able to approximate, and in some moments reenact, the potent atmosphere of that heritage–an atmosphere that remains, in part, inaccessible to many Anglophone readers.

Third, from the point of view of the English-language poet–particularly one who has already undertaken the immense effort required to familiarize oneself with the English poetic tradition–Mashriqi English offers an opportunity to infuse Arabic and Persianate themes into their verse without compromising the meanings and usages of the original words through ill-suited translations. Certain concepts and phonological shapes in these legacy languages are simply irreproducible in English–through no fault of English itself, but as a natural consequence of distinct cultural, religious, and civilizational trajectories. The Mashriqi English poet may be able to remedy this expressive gap by skillfully incorporating Perso-Arabic terms into their work, much as Urdu poets in earlier periods did–and continue to do today.

I believe that Mashriqi English will be justified not by the academic arguments presented here, but by those hoped-for creatives who will employ it to fashion new chords of feeling and expression–to set into poetry what "it would impoverish us to forget," to quote Robert Frost. Ultimately, however, it will be the discerning reader–and their perceptive taste–who will determine whether Mashriqi English rises or sinks as a novel medium of expression.

How to Write Mashriqi English: Guiding Principles

There are no strict rules for writing poetry in Mashriqi English; however, the following general principles may guide the poet in choosing vocabulary and expressions in a coherent and effective manner.

Word Choice

◇ Mashriqi English is rooted in Modern Standard English and should not deviate from its accepted grammatical structures or core vocabulary. Its Anglo-Arabic script is based on the pronunciation of General American English.

◇ Only words of Arabic or Persian derivation may be incorporated into Mashriqi English. Terms of other origins–such as Turkic or Indic–may be used if they are already attested in Arabic or Persian, or if they are contextually relevant to the subject matter.

◇ Arabic and Persian words should retain their historical meanings and reflect their usage in languages such as Urdu, Chagatai, Ottoman Turkish, and other culturally and literarily related traditions. Arabic terms not attested in Persian are best avoided.

◇ The categories of Perso-Arabic words to be incorporated into Mashriqi English should reflect vocabulary that expresses concepts–whether elevated or mundane–related to culture, love, emotion, art, religion, science, and the mystical experience, preferably with antecedents in Urdu, the Turkic language family, and other culturally related languages. These are what we may call emblematic or iconic words: signposts for layers of meaning and usage already established and understood in the source languages and their cultural relatives. It is best to avoid replacing basic English vocabulary (such as pronouns, particles, and auxiliary verbs) with Arabic or Persian terms, focusing instead on "learnèd" words. Nevertheless, there is no imperative to replace any particular English term–whether of Germanic, French, Latin, or Greek origin–with a Perso-Arabic equivalent. Any English or Perso-Arabic word may be used if it serves the context.

◇ In the same vein, Arabic and Persian words must remain generally true to their original forms, pronunciation, and spelling in the Perso-Arabic script. The recommended guide to pronunciation is Classical Persian–not modern Western Persian. This includes the *majhūl* vowels ē and ō, the diphthongs *ay* and *aw*, and the retention of final *-a*. The details are explained in the introduction to Anglo-Arabic script.

◇ Wholesale, indiscriminate replacement of English vocabulary with Perso-Arabic terms is not advised.

Grammar

◇ As stated previously, Mashriqi English is first and foremost English and must remain rooted in modern English grammar and usage.

◇ Arabic broken plurals can be used (*kitāb, kutub,* "book, books"), as well as regular plurals in -īn and -āt (*muʾmin, muʾminīn* "believer, believers"; *kalima, kalimāt,* "word, words"). The Arabic dual *-ayn* can be used where it occurs in the source languages (e.g. Urdu *wālidayn* "parents").

Additionally, Perso-Arabic words may be used without a plural suffix if they occur in a collective or generic sense.

◇ Arabic and Persian words can receive the English *-s* plural suffix (pronounced *s* or *z* according the voicedness of the final consonant), as well as the Persian *-hā* and *-ān* plural suffixes (*muʾmins, muʾminān, muʾminhā* "believers").

◇ The Persian *izāfat* (the suffix *-i*) is exclusively used with Perso-Arabic words: (1) to attach two nouns, where the possessed occurs before the possessor (*kitāb-i Ahmad*, "Ahmad's book"), and (2) to connect a noun to its post-posed adjective (*kitāb-i surkh*, "red book"). However, the *izāfat* is not obligatory and the usual English possessive structures and word order may be employed: *Ahmad's kitāb, the kitāb of Ahmad, surkh kitāb.*

◇ Perso-Arabic adjectives may precede or follow the noun, whether Perso-Arabic or English. When following a Perso-Arabic noun, it is preferable to use the Persian *izāfat* construction, a short *-i* tacked onto the pre-posed noun.

◇ Although few Perso-Arabic verbs have been employed in this collection, the general principle is that Perso-Arabic verbs, nouns, and adjectives may be used without modification as English verbs (*sulūk*, "behavior" as noun or "behave" as verb). This follows historical English precedent, where nouns and adjectives have become verbs without changing their form, and are conjugated like regular English verbs. The regular past tense suffix may be written as *-ed,* '*ed*, *-d* or attached directly to the stem (*sulūk*-ed, *sulūk'*ed, *sulūk*ed, *sulūk'*d, "behaved"). I have experimented with specific Persian-derived verbalizing suffixes, such as *-kar* and *-kun* (e.g. *sulūkkar* or *sulūkkun*), and future writers might attempt to find their own suffixes.

◇ Perso-Arabic must take the definite and indefinite articles as if they were native English words (the *nay*–not bare *nay* as in Persian, and *ishq*–like *love*–with no definite article). Similarly, it is advisable to pluralize a Perso-Arabic word where its English equivalent would be plural in the same context.

◇ It is hoped that poetry written in Mashriqi English will be well-crafted and stand on its own merits. This means that it should take into account precedents in the English poetic tradition like meter, rhyme, literary devices, and the interplay between sound and meaning. More importantly, it is hoped that poets will be creatively attuned to the works of their predecessors, whether in English, Arabic, or Persian. Our aim is to produce good poetry first–Mashriqi English poetry second.

26

The Anglo-Arabic Alphabet

Introduction

The Anglo-Arabic alphabet is derived from the Perso-Arabic alphabet, which in turn is based on the Arabic script with additional letters to represent Persian sounds not present in Arabic. The Anglo-Arabic alphabet will be familiar to readers of languages that use Perso-Arabic-based alphabets such as Urdu, Punjabi, Sindhi, Sorani Kurdish, Pashto, Balochi, and many others. It is also closely related to historical forms of the Arabic script including the Ottoman Turkish, Chagatai, and Jawi alphabets. The Anglo-Arabic alphabet follows all the conventions of the Arabic script, including right-to-left direction and positional letter forms.

Mashriqi English utilizes the letters and diacritics of the Arabic script to represent the consonants and vowels of Perso-Arabic as well as English words. Seven additional letters—four consonants and two vowels—represent sounds not found in Arabic. Four of the consonants—گ ژ چ پ (/g/, /ʒ/, /tʃ/, and /p/, respectively)—are borrowed from Persian, while the fifth, ڤ /v/, is derived from Arabic ف /f/. The two additional vowel letters are ێ /eː/ and ۏ /oː/.

Perso-Arabic-descended words preserve their original spellings except in a few cases involving the Classical Persian *majhūl* vowels (ē and ō) and medial *hamzah*. When writing Mashriqi English in Latin script, standard American English spelling is used, while Perso-Arabic words, always italicized, are romanized according to the table below.

Vowels

The vowels of Mashriqi English are based on the phonology of General American English, Classical Arabic, and Classical Persian and are represented with three Arabic vowel letters (و ي ا)–either basic or augmented with diacritics–and four additional diacritics (ٰ ّ ٔ ـ) that occur above and below consonants. Some vowels are unique to English words, some occur in both English and Perso-Arabic words, while two (ē and ō) occur exclusively in Persian-origin words.

General Guidelines

◇ As in Perso-Arabic script, word-initial vowels are "carried" by an *alif*, as in أدب (*adab* "literature; manners") where the initial *fatḥah*, double *fatḥah*, *ḍammah* or *kasrah* is carried by the *alif*. The *alif* also precedes the long vowels represented by *wāw* and *yāʾ*; initial ā is rendered آ, an *alif* topped by a *maddah*.

◇ Similar to Persian, the *hamzah* (ء) does not occur above or underneath an initial *alif*, but may occur medially in some words, where it follows Arabic spelling. Even in medial positions, it may be replaced by *yāʾ* (ي) or *wāw* (و) in certain words: e.g., Arabic سؤال (*suʾāl* "question") becomes سوال (*suwāl*) in Mashriqi English; compare Urdu *sawāl*.

◇ The so-called short vowels indicated by *fatḥah*, double *fatḥah*, *ḍammah*, and *kasrah* (´ ، ˝ ، ˏ) are optional, unless they are necessary to distinguish homographs where context is unclear. In this collection they are frequently–but not consistently–employed for clarity.

◇ As in the Perso-Arabic alphabet, the *matres lectionis* و and ي (*wāw* and *yāʾ*) function both as the vowels /u/ and /i/, and as the consonants /w/ and /j/.

◇ The Classical Persian *majhūl* vowels ē and ō are pronounced according to their historical values /eː/ and /oː/–retained in modern Dari Persian and Urdu, unlike Western Persian. In poetry, they are treated as equivalent to the English diphthongs /eɪ/ and /oʊ/ and are represented with the same Anglo-Arabic letters. Thus, English *maze* and Persian *mēz* (table) become homographs (میز) and are considered rhymes. Similarly, the vowel in English *ghost* (گوست) and in Persian *gōsht* (گوشت) is represented with the same letter and treated as equivalent in poetic contexts.

◇ As in Arabic but unlike Persian, final *yāʾ* retains its two lower dots. For example, علي (*Alī*) in Anglo-Arabic and Arabic, but علی in Persian and Urdu.

◇ The Persian *izāfat* is a short, unstressed vowel that links a head noun with a following noun or adjective. As in Persian and Urdu, it is marked with a *kasrah* (ِ) under the last letter of the head noun and is transliterated *-i* or *-yi* after a vowel. The pronunciation corresponds to the vowel of English *bit* or the final reduced vowel of *happy*. This is in keeping with Classical Persian, and unlike Western Persian, where the *izāfat* is pronounced *-e*. E.g., مي عِشـق (*may-i ishq* "the wine of love").

◇ In Perso-Arabic compounds, a short *-u-* may connect two or more nouns and is written و in Anglo-Arabic. It is pronounced like the vowel in English *put* (/ʊ/); e.g., خار و خون (*khār-u-khūn*, "thorns and blood").

◇ The mid central short vowel known as schwa (/ə/) is rendered ë in the romanization of Persian reduplicative compounds such as *justëjū* "diligent search" and *guftëgū* "conversation, speech." It also occurs in the Persian nouns *āshënā* "lover; companion"; *ārëzū* "wish, desire"; and *āsëmān* "sky, heaven"; where it is pronounced or elided (thus yielding *āshnā*, etc., and resulting in a reduced syllable) based on metrical considerations. In English words, it is represented with a double *fathah* (ً; e.g. فاذَر /faðər/), which also represents the vowel of English *shut* (شَت /ʃʌt/).

◇ Initial consonant clusters are not found in Classical Arabic or Persian. In English words, the first letter of a two-consonant cluster or the first two letters of a three-consonant cluster either bear a *sukūn* (ْ) or are left unmarked; e.g.

سکرپ or سُکْرَپ *scrap*. The same rule applies in reverse to final clusters; e.g., *fast* is فَسْت or فست.

◇ Arabic *tanwīn*, or nunation, does not occur in Mashriqi English except in word-final positions in certain Arabic-derived adverbs such as لطفاً (*lutfan* "please") or خصوصاً (*khusūsan* "especially"). It is represented with an *alif* bearing a double *fathah*, and is unrelated in function or value to the word-medial double *fathah* mentioned above.

Anglo-Arabic Letters

The table below presents Anglo-Arabic letters alongside their English, Romanized Perso-Arabic, and IPA equivalents. Positional forms follow Perso-Arabic convention and will not be indicated.

Anglo-Arabic	Name	English	Romanized Perso-Arabic	IPA
ء	همزه *hamza*			ʔ
ا	الف *alif*	a	a, ā	æ ɑ(ː) ʔ
آ	الف مدّه *alif-i madda*	a	ā	ɑ(ː)
ب	با *bā*	b	b	b

پ	*pā* پا	p	p	p
ت	*tā* تا	t	t	t
ث	*thā* ثا	th	th	θ
ج	*jīm* جيم	j	j	dʒ
چ	*chīm* چيم	ch	ch	tʃ
ح	*hē* حي	h	h	h
خ	*khā* خا	kh	kh	x
د	*dāl* دال	d	d	d
ذ	*dhāl* ذال	th	dh	ð
ر	*rā* را	r	r	r
ز	*zā* زا	z	z	z
ژ	*zhā* ژا	s, z	zh	ʒ
س	*sīn* سين	s	s	s
ش	*shīn* شين	sh	sh	ʃ
ص	*sād* صاد	s	s	s
ض	*zād* ضاد	z	z	z
ط	*tē* طي	t	t	t
ظ	*zē* ظي	z	z	z
ع	*ayn* عين		ʿ	ʔ
غ	*ghayn* غين		gh	ɣ
ف	*fā* فا	f	f	f
ق	*qāf* قاف		q	q
ك	*kāf* كاف	k	k	k
گ	*gāf* گاف	g	g	g
ل	*lām* لام	l	l	l
م	*mīm* ميم	m	m	m
ن	*nūn* نون	n	n	n

و	واو *wāw*	w	w	w
ؤ	واوِ همزه *wāw-i hamza*		o	ɔ ɑ
وَ	واوِ مدّه *wāw-i madda*		ō	oː
ه	ها *hā*	h	h	h
ي	يا *yā*	y	y	j
ئ	ياي مدّه *yā-yi hamza*	e	e	ɛ
ـَي	ياي مدّه *yā-yi madda*		ē	eː

Anglo-Arabic Diacritics

Diacritic	Name	IPA
´	*fatḥah*	æ
˝	double *fatḥah*	ə (when unstressed) ʌ (when stressed)
´	*ḍammah*	ʊ
˛	*kasrah*	ɪ
˝	*shaddah*	geminates consonants
˚	*sukūn*	indicates no vowel after a consonant

English Sounds and Their Anglo-Arabic Equivalents

The first example is an English word while the second is a Perso-Arabic word.

English IPA	Anglo-Arabic Script	Romanized Perso-Arabic	Examples	
ɑ	آ،ا	ā	فاذر آب	father *āb* water (poetic, literary)
æ	ـَ	a	لَند بَند	land *band* closed
eɪ	ـَي		لیَت	late
eː	ـَي	ē	میَز	*mēz* table
æɪ	ـَي	ay	دَیر	*dayr* monastery
ɛ	ئ	e	بئد	bed
ɛɹ	ـَیر		کیَرد	cared
i	ي	ī	بیت گیتي	beat *gītī* world

ɪ	ِ	i	بِت هِند	bit *Hind* India
ɪɹ	ِر	ir	مِرّر سِرّ	mirror *sirr* secret
aɪ	آي، اي	āy	كراي آينه	cry *āyīna* mirror
ɑɹ	آر، ار	ār	كار آرام	car *ārām* calm, quiet
ɔɹ	ـَور	ōr	كَور گَور	core *gōr* grave
ɔ, ɑ	ـؤ		كؤت لؤت	caught lot
oʊ	ـَو		كَول	coal
oː	ـَو	ō	رَوز	*rōz* day
ɔɪ	ـَوي	oy	بَوي خَوي	boy *khoy* (also *khūy*) humor, nature
ʊ	ُ	u	بُك گُل	book *kull* all, totality
ʊɹ	ـُر	ur	كُرّنت دُرّ	current *durr* pearl

u	و	ū	پول	pool
			پول	*pūl* money
aʊ	آو	āw	کاو	cow
	ـو	aw	گاو	*gāw* cow
			دَولت	*dawlat* state, country; wealth
ʌ	´		گَت	cut
ɜɹ	ـر		وَرلد	world
ə	´	ë (only in certain Persian words)	کِچُن	kitchen
			گفتگو	*guftëgū* conversation
			آسِمان	*āsëmān* sky
əɹ	ـر		مَذَر	mother

Consonants

◇ The values of Anglo-Arabic letters are detailed in the table below. The following points should be taken into consideration:

◇ Perso-Arabic *wāw*, when used as a consonant, is always rendered *w* and never *v*, as the former is more in line with the Arabic, Classical Persian, and English pronunciation.

◇ As in the Perso-Arabic alphabet, the *matres lectionis* (*wāw* and *yāʾ*) function both as the vowels /u/ and /i/, and as the consonants /w/ and /j/.

◇ In some Arabic-derived words the final *tāʾ marbūṭah* (ة) is rendered ه (romanized as *-a*), without dots, as in Persian; e.g. ترجمه (*tarjuma* "translation"). In other cases, also following Persian convention, it becomes a final *t*; e.g. روایت (*riwāyat* "narrative").

◇ Since /θ/ and /ð/ are found in both English and Arabic, they are represented by the equivalent Arabic letters ث and ذ, respectively. They are never rendered as *s* and *z*, as is common in Persian, Urdu, Turkish, and other related languages.

◇ Mashriqi English follows Persian in rendering ص as *s*, ط as *t*, ض and ظ as *z*, ح as *h*, and ع as ʿ (pronounced as a glottal stop), since these sounds are not found in English. However, the reader may give them their Arabic pronunciation if they wish.

◇ In Perso-Arabic romanization, Arabic ʿayn and *hamzah* are not written at the beginning of words but are indicated medially and finally with an apostrophe: عین *ayn* "eye; same" but سَعْي *saʾy* "search, effort." In many cases, final *hamzah* is dropped, whereas final ʿ*ayn* is not omitted.

◇ By contrast, the Perso-Arabic ق (/q/) is pronounced—as it is in Urdu and Uzbek, for example—and rendered as *q* in romanization.

◇ Similarly, the pronunciation of Perso-Arabic /x/ (خ) and /ɣ/ (غ) is maintained.

◇ When transcribing the English plural or possessive, /s/ and /z/ are represented with س and ز respectively, depending on whether the preceding consonant is voiceless or voiced. After vowels, /z/ (ز) is always used. When writing in the English alphabet, the usual convention is followed.

◇ Similarly, when transcribing the regular English past tense, -ed is rendered either as ت (/-t/) or د (/-d/) depending on whether the previous consonant is voiceless or voiced. After vowels, it is always د (/-d/). When the past tense suffix is /-ɪd/, it is written د with a previous *kasrah* to indicate the short, or lenis, vowel.

The first example is an English word while the second is a Perso-Arabic word.

English IPA	Anglo-Arabic Script	Conventional English/ Romanized Perso-Arabic	Examples
m	م	m	مَذَر mother *mādar* مادر mother (poetic, literary)
n	ن	n	نون noon *nān* نان bread
b	ب	b	بارد bard *bāda* باده wine
p	پ	p	پَن pan *pīr* پیر spiritual guide
f	ف	f	فار far *fard* فَرد individual

v	ف	v	فَست vast
w	و	w	وقَل wall *wāsita* واسطه means, medium
θ	ث	th	ثِن thin *thābit* ثابت firm
ð	ذ	th, dh	ذَت that *dhāt* ذات self
t	ت	t	تَن tan *tan* تَن body
d	د	d	دوت dot *dam* دَم breath, moment
s	س	s	سیَل sale *sabab* سبب reason

z	ز	z	زئست zest *zōr* زور hard
ʃ	ش	sh	شِپ ship *shōr* شوَر noise
ʒ	ژ	s, z, zh	مِژَّر measure *zhāla* ژاله dew
tʃ	چ	ch	چُرچ church *chāy* چاي tea
dʒ	ج	j	جَم jam جُستجو *justējū* diligent search
r	ر	r	رَم ram *rind* رِند a Sufi affecting debauchery

ŋ ng	نگ	ng	کِنگ *king* فِنگر *finger* *tang* تَنگ distressed
k	ك	k	گَندْل candle or گَندّل *kāmil* کامل whole, perfect
g	گ	g	گَیم game *gum* گُم lost, missing
x	خ	kh	*Khudā* خُدا God
ɣ	غ	gh	*gham* غَم sadness, grief
ʔ	ع، ء		*dam'a* دمعه tear *qirā'at* قراءت recitation (of the Qur'an)

q	ق	q	*qadar* قدر destiny
h	ه	h	هوم home *āhang* آهنگ melody, tune
j	ي	y	يئلو yellow *yār* يار friend, companion, lover
w	و	w	وئل well *wādī* وادي valley

Khayt-i Zarīn (The Golden Thread)

The *khayt-i zarīn*
we're called to uncover.
The *jild* of the ālim,
the *khatt* of the lover.

The *shi'r* of tomorrow,
āwāz of the past.
The Sūfī's sweet *nay*,
both sober and *mast*.

It runs through our tales,
this *shāhāna* thread.
Like ornate *zardōzī*,
in golden and red.

It binds our *thaqāfat*s
with our *farhang*s.
And blends our *qasā'id*
with *dāstān*s and *rang*s.

Be this our effort,
to straighten the *rāh*
whereby the *gadā*
might rise as *pādshāh*.

Glossary

khayt-i zarīn golden thread.
jild volume, tome, bound book.
ālim scholar, savant.
khatt letter.
shi'r poetry.
āwāz voice.
nay (reed) flute.
mast (spiritually) intoxicated.
shāhāna royal, kingly.
zardōzī gold(en) embroidery.
thaqāfat (Arabic) culture.

farhang (Persian) culture.
qasā'id plural of *qasīda* long-form poem.
dāstān fable, romance, tale.
rang color; type, sort.
rāh way, path; manner.
gadā beggar; spiritual seeker.
pādshāh king, emperor, sovereign.

خیط زرین (ذہ گوَلدن ثرئد)

ذہ خیط زرین
ویر کوَلد تو اَنکڤر.
ذہ جلد اڤ ذہ عالم،
ذہ خط اڤ ذہ لڤر.

ذہ شِعر اڤ تُمؤرو،
آواز اڤ ذہَ پست
ذہ صوفیز سویت نی،
بوَث سوَبرَ اندَ مست.

اِت رَّنز ثرو آر تیلز
ذِس شاهانه ثرئد.
لایک اوَرنیت زردوَزِي،
اِن گوَلدن انَد رئد.

اِت بایندز آر ثقافتس
وِث آور فرهنگز
اَند بلئندز آر قصائد
وِث داستانز َاند رنگز.

بي ذس آر ائڤرت
تو ستریَتن ذہ راہ
ویَرباي ذَہ گدا
مایت رایز از پادشاہ.

In the Mughal Garden

In lush *bāghīcha*s brimming full
Of blooming *phūl* and fragrant *gul.*

Where *khushbū* bled by young *kalīs*
Is stolen by the evening breeze.

Therein I sought to drink my fill
Of playful eyes that tease then kill.

The *bāghbān* said, "my wretched son
We know who's lost, and who has won.

Soft hearts can't challenge swift gazelles
Or hope to conquer *maghrūr* belles.

Your Majnūn's fate was always clear
The moment Laylā shot her *tīr!*"

Glossary

bāghīcha a small garden in
which flowers, fruits, or
vegetables are grown.
phūl (Urdu) flower(s).
gul flower(s).

khushbū fragrant, fragrance.
kalī (Urdu) blossom, bud.
bāghbān gardener.
maghrūr proud, vain.
tīr arrow.

اِن ذَه مُغل گاردن

ان لَش باغیچَز برِمنگ فُل
اف بلومنگ پھول آند فرَیگرنت گل

وَیر خوشبو بلئد باي یَنگ کلیز
اِز ستوَلن باي ذه ایڤنگ بریز.

ذَیر اِن آي سؤت تو درِنك ماي فَل
اف پلیَیفُل آیز ذت تیز ذئن کِل.

ذه باغبان سئد، "ماي رئچِد سَّن
وي نوَ ھوز لؤست، اَند ھو ھَز وَّن.

سؤفت ھارتس کنت چَلِنج سْوِفت غزئلز
اوَر ھوَپ تو کؤنگر مغرور بئلز.

یوَر مجنونز فیَت وَّز اوَلوِیَز کلیر
ذَه موَمنت لیلی شوَت ھَر تیر."

Shāyad (Perhaps)

I hope you'll miss me when I'm gone, perhaps.
Or will you blithely carry on, perhaps?

You tore my shirt like Yūsuf's from the back.
You meant to rip my *garēbān*, perhaps?

I heard my *yār* denied our *ishq* three times.
I've ended up as some "*fulān*," perhaps.

So slim, so lithe, with *gēsūs* black and wild.
Quite worth the loss of one's *īmān*, perhaps?

You left Mahzūn beneath a weeping sky.
We'll meet amid the *kahkashān*–perhaps!

Glossary

Mahzūn "The Saddened One." The poet's *takhallus*, i.e. pen name. It is customary to include the *takhallus* in the last couplet of a ghazal.
shāyad perhaps.
garēbān collar.

yār lover, friend, companion.
ishq love, passion.
fulān so-and-so person, stranger.
gēsū curl, lock, ringlet.
īmān faith, belief.
kahkashān galaxy, milky way.

شاید (پَرهَپس)

آي هۆپ يول مِس مي وئن آيم گۆن، پَّرهَپس.
اۆر وِل يو بلايذلي گَري اؤن، پرَهَپس؟

يو تۆر ماي شَّرت لايك يوسُفس فرَم ذه بَك.
يو مئنت تو رِپ ماي گريبان، پرَهَپس؟

آي هُرد ماي يار دِنايد آر عِشْق ثري تايمز.
آيف ائندد اَپ از سَّم ”فُلان“، پرَهَپس؟

سَو سُلِم، سَو لايذ، وِث گَيسوز بُلك اند وايلد.
كوايت وَرث ذه لؤس اڤ ونز ايمان، پرَهَپس؟

يو لئفت محزون بِنيث اه ويپنگ سُكاي.
ويل ميت اَمِد ذه كهكشان-پرَهَپس؟

The Scorpion and the Turtle

A scorpion's legs were stuck in bankside mud
Awaiting drowning death in storm and flood.

Just then he saw a turtle edging past
Who moved quite slow but rode the waters fast.

The mud-bound one, with courtliest behavior
Addressed himself to his potential savior.

"Oh noble one, have mercy for my life
For as you see this downpour's brought me strife

A heart such as your own is far too kind
To coldly leave a drowning soul behind

Indeed, the *jangal* knows your reputation
As most humane among the Lord's creation

By taking me to safety and *salāmat*
You'll score some ready points for your *qiyāmat*

And once we jointly cross this raging *nahr*
You'll gain a servant till the end of *dahr!*"

The turtle, not naïve to jungle-living
Explained in careful words his grave misgiving.

He said, "I feel for your *kambakht* ordeal
But still I must insist we have no deal.

I'll speak with frankness tempered with sound reason:
A rogue such as yourself is primed for treason

Before my feet imprint the other bank
You'll surely plunge your stinger in my flank!"

Replied the scorpion, "*shaykhī*, you are right
But that was well before I saw the light

Now that my future days and nights depend
Upon your grace my villainy will end

My own self-interest lies in your survival
And in our wholesome riverbank arrival."

The floundering arachnid glibly pleaded
Until the testudine at length conceded.

With scorpion balanced on his steady shell
He swam and struggled with the angry swell.

But as the shore appeared—to his surprise
Or not—he felt a sting between his eyes!

The turtle, dying, gasped, "you blasted knave
Your act has doomed us to a silty grave!"

He then exclaimed "to your *zamīr* you swore
To check your instinct till we reached the shore!"

Explained the scorpion in his dying breath
"My vows are faithless even unto death

Your doubts about my nature were all true
As scorpions are, so scorpions surely do."

Glossary

jangal jungle.
salāmat safety.
qiyāmat Day of Resurrection
and Judgment.
nahr river.

dahr eon, long period of time;
fate.
kambakht unlucky, unfortunate.
shaykhī my teacher, my guide.
zamīr conscience.

ذه سکۏرپیَن اند ذه تَّرتل

اہ سکۏرپیَنز لئگز وَّر ستَك ان بِنکساید مد
اویَننگ دراوننگ دئث ان ستۏرم اَند فلَد.

جُست ذئن هي سؤ اہ تَّرتل ائجنگ پَست
هو موۏد کوایْت سلۏ بَت رۏد ذه وؤتَّرز فَست.

ذه مَّد باونت وَّن، وِث کۏرتلیَّست بهیَثیَّر
ادرئست هِمسئلف تو هِز پتئنشل سیَثیَّر.

”اۏ نۏبل وَّن، هڤ مَّرسي فۏر ماي لايف
فۏر از یو سي ذیز داونپۏرز برؤت مي سترايف

اہ هارت سَّج اَز یۏر اۏن اِز فار تو کايند
تو کۏلدلي لیڤ اہ دراوننگ سۏل بِهايند

اِندید، ذه جنگل نوز یۏر رِپیُتیَّشن
اَز موست هویمیَن امَّنگ ذه لۏردز کریَیَّشن

باي تیَکنگ مي تو سیَفتي اند سلامت
یول سکۏر سَّم رئدي پۏینتس فۏر یۏر قیامت

اند وَّنس وي جۏینتلي کرۏس ذِس ریَجنگ نهْر
یول گیَن اہ سَّرڤنت تِل ذه ائند اڤ دهْرا!“

54

ذه تَّرتل، نؤت نايييڤ تو جنگل لِڤنگ
ائكسپليَند ان كيَرفُل وَردز هِز گرِيڤ مسِگِڤنگ.

هي سئد، "آي فيل ڤوَر يور كمبَخت اوَرديل
بَت سُتِل آي مَست اِنسِست وي هڤ نوَ ديل.

آيل سپيك وِث فرنكنس تئمپرد وث ساوند ريزن:
اه روَگ سَچ أز يوَرسئل اِز پرايمد ڤوَر تريزْن

بِڤوَر ماي فيت اِمپرِنت ذه أذر بنك
يول شُرلي پلَنج يوَر سْتِنگر ان ماي ڤلنك!"

رِپلايد ذه سكوَرپِين، "شيخي، يو آر رايت
بَت ذت وَز وئل بِڤوَر آي سؤ ذه لايت

ناو ذت ماي فيوچر ديَز اند نايتس دِپئند
أپوَن يوَر گريَس ماي ڤِلني وِل ائند

ماي اوَن سئلف انترست لايز ان يور سَرڤايڤل
اند اِن آر هوَلسم رِڤربند ارايڤل."

ذه فلاوندرنگ اركُند گِلبلي پليدِد
انتل ذه تئستيَداين ات لئنگث گَنسيدِد.

وِث سكوَرپيَن بلَنست اؤن هِز ستئدي شئل
هي سْوَم اند سْتْرَگلد وث ذه انگري سْوئل.

بَت اَز ذه شوَر اپيرد – تو هِز سَرپرايز
اوَر نؤت – هي فئلت اه سْتِنگ بِتوين هِز آيز!

ذه ترتل، دايننگ، گسپت، "يو بْلَستد نيَّف
يوَر اكت هَز دومد اَس تو اه سِلتي گرِيَّف!"

هي ذئن ائكسكليَمد، "تو يور ضمير يو سْووَر
تو چئك يوَر انسْتِنكت تِل وي ريچد ذه شوَر!"

ائكسپليَّند ذه سكوَرپيَّن اِن هِز دايننگ برئث
"ماي ڤاوز آز فيَّثلس ايڤن اَنتو دئث

يوَر داوتس اَباوت ماي نيَّچر ور اؤل ترو
اَز سكوَرپيَّنز آر، سو سكوَرپيَّنز دو."

Dīda (My Eye)

No sleep relieves my *dīda* through these long and lonely
nights.
The *hudhud* lies *khwābīda* through these long and lonely
nights.

My carefree heart that used to take delight in your reproach
Has slowly grown *sanjīda* through these long and lonely
nights.

Could it have been the burden of entombing our *hawā*
That made my back *khamīda* through these long and
lonely nights?

One evening twenty years ago your scent embraced my
shawq
And kept me *yād-khandīda* through these long and lonely
nights.

World-worshippers crave *shān* and fame *magar* Mahzūn has
heaped
Awrāq-i khizān-dīda through these long and lonely nights.

Glossary

Mahzūn "The Saddened One."
The poet's *takhallus*, i.e. pen
name. It is customary to include
the *takhallus* in the last couplet
of a ghazal.
dīda eye, vision, sight.
hudhud hoopoe.
khwābīda sleeping, slumbering.
sanjīda serious, grave.
hawā desire, passion; longing,
attachment.

khamīda bent.
shawq longing, yearning.
yād-khandīda smiling at
memories.
shān glory, authority, power.
magar but, however; only.
awrāq-i khizān-dīda autumn-
withered pages/leaves.

ديده (ماي آي)

نوَ سليپ رِليفَز ماي ديده ثرو ذيز لؤنگ أَند لوَنلي نايتس.
ذه هُدهُد لايز خوابيده ثرو ذيز لؤنگ أَند لوَنلي نايتس.

ماي كَيرفري هارت ذت يوزد تو تيَك دِلايت ان يور رِپرِچ
هَز سلوَلي گروَن سنجيده ثرو ذيز لؤنگ أَند لوَنلي نايتس.

كُد ات هَڤ بِن ذه بُردن اڤ اِنتومنگ آور هوى
ذت مَيد ماي بَك خميده ثرو ذيز لؤنگ أَند لوَنلي نايتس.

ين ايڤننگ توئنتي ييرز اگوَ يور سِئنت امبرِيَست ماي شَوق
اند كئپت مي يادخنديده ثرو ذيز لؤنگ اند لوَنلي نايتس.

وَرلد وَرشِپَرز كرِيَف شان اند فيَم مگر محزون هَز هيپت
اوراقِ خزانديده ثرو ذيز لؤنگ أَند لوَنلي نايتس.

Tāq (The Wall Cove)

Take heed, for *ishq* has lost its way, take heed.
And *āshiq*s shall be forced to pay, take heed.

My *kūza*'s shattered into countless shards.
The *kūzagar*'s become his clay, take heed.

When Laylā's father gave a grudging "yes"
Majnūn decided not to stay, take heed.

An eyebrow-less *qalandar* wandered nude.
Makhmūr without a drop of *may*, take heed.

You filled your *tāq* with dusty books, Mahzūn
The soul has nothing left to say, take heed.

Glossary

Mahzūn "The Saddened One." The poet's *takhallus*, i.e. pen name. It is customary to include the *takhallus* in the last couplet of a ghazal.
ishq (divine; extreme, all-consuming) love, passion.
āshiq lover, person afflicted with *ishq*.
kūza a type of earthenware.

kūzagar potter.
qalandar a Sufi itinerant who resounces the material aspects of life.
makhmūr (spiritually) intoxicated.
may wine.
tāq cove in the wall in traditional homes.

طاق (ذه وؤل كوَڤ)

تيَك هيد، فوَر عِشق هِز لؤست هز ويَ، تيَك هيد.
اَند عاشقس شل بي فوَرست تو يَ، تيَك هيد.

ماي كوزَز شَتَّرد اِنتو كاونتلس شاردز.
ذه كوزگرز بِگَم هِز كليَ، تيَك هيد.

وئن ليلاز فاذر گيَف أه گُرَّجنگ "يئس"
مجنون دِسايدِد نؤت تو ستيَ، تيَك هيد.

أه آيبراو-لِس قَلَنَدَر وؤندرَّد نود
مخمور وِذاوت اه درؤپ اڤ مَي، تيَك هيد.

يو فِلد يور طاق وِث دَستي بُكس، محزون
ذه سوَل هَز نَّثِنگ لئفت تو سي، تيَك هيد.

Īd

Tomorrow's Īd-i Ramazān—let *sharāb* break our fast.
How can I face you at the *bazm* unless I'm soundly *mast*?

How can I *bardāsht zindagī*—how can I bear these sins?
How can I sow tomorrow's seed stuck in a barren past?

Remember when you swore "I'll never leave your *shirīn* side"?
Remember when we spent that fleeting summer *dast dar dast*?

We turned some heads and raised a few *mahabhat-sitēz* brows.
But little did I know I'd be declared the town's outcast.

When I was young the seers said "he'll never fall in love!"
The *jādūgar*s deserve a lash for every spell they cast.

Fair-weather friend, I do not need your shame and *malāmat*.
Ārē! Mahzūn's the first to know *afsāna*s never last!

Glossary

Mahzūn "The Saddened One." The poet's *takhallus*, i.e. pen name. It is customary to include the *takhallus* in the last couplet of a ghazal.

Īd-i Ramazān Eid al-Fitr, the Islamic festival marking the end of Ramadan.

sharāb wine.

bazm party, assembly, feast.

mast intoxicated, drunk.

bardāsht bear, tolerate.

zindagī life.

shirīn sweet.

dast dar dast hand in hand, holding hands.

mahabhat-sitēz love-hating, hostile to love.

jādūgar sorcerer, sorceress.

malāmat reproach.

ārē yes, truly, indeed.

afsāna fairy tales, stories.

عيد

تَمؤروَز عيدِ رضمان – لئت شَراب برِيَك آر فَست.
هاو گَن آي فِيَس يو اَت ذُه بزْم أَنلئس آيم ساوندلي مَست؟

هاو گَن آي برداشت زِندگِي – هاو كان آي بيَر ذيز سنز؟
هاو گَن آي سوَ تَمؤروَز سيد سْتَّك اِن اه بَرْن پست؟

رِمئمبر وئن يو سوَوَر "آيل نئثر لِيف يور شِرين سايد؟"
رِمئمبر وئن وي سپئنت ذت فليتنگ سَمر دست در دست؟

وي تَرند سَّم هئدز اند رِيَزد اه فيو محبت سِتيَز براوز.
بَت لِتل دِد آي نوَ آيد بي دِكليَرد ذه تاونز آوتكَسْت.

وئن آي وَّز يَنگ ذه سِيَّرز سئد "هيل نئثر فؤل ان لَڤ!"
ذه جادوگرز دِزَرِف اه لِش فوَر ائثري سپئل ذيَ گَست.

فيَر وئذر فرئند، آي دو نؤت نيد يور شيَم اند ملامت.
آريَ! محزونز ذه فَرست تو نوَ افسائَز نئثر لَسْت!

The Flame of *Fanā* (Annihilation)

For *kashmīr* cloth and jewels we do not care
For people's *rasm* and rules we do not care.

We moths will spiral into *fanā*'s flame.
You say we're frenzied fools? We do not care.

This *ālam*'s fickle like the *barsāt* months.
It scorches then it cools—we do not care.

The path of *haqq* is fraught with *khār-u-khūn*.
We wrestle *dēws* and *ghūls*—we do not care.

Uff! Let them laugh and say Mahzūn has joined
A *halqa* of *Bahlūls*—we do not care!

Glossary

Mahzūn "The Saddened One." The poet's *takhallus*, i.e. pen name. It is customary to include the *takhallus* in the last couplet of a ghazal.
kashmīr cashmere, an expensive type of cloth.
rasm custom, tradition; drawing.
fanā spiritual annihilation, annihilation of the self.
ālam (material) world.
barsāt the rainy, monsoon season of the Indian Subcontinent.

haqq truth.
khār-u-khūn thorns and blood.
dēw dēv, a demon from Persian mythology.
ghūl ghoul, a monster from Arabian mythology.
uff uff, an exclamation of exasperation or frustration.
halqa a circle of mystics or suchlike.
Bahlūl Bahlūl epithet of Wahab ibn ʿAmr, a historical figure who feigned madness to speak truth to power.

ذه فليَم اڤ فينا (انايليشن)

فوَر كشمير كلؤث اند جولز وي دو نؤت كيَر
فوَر پيپلز رسُم اند رولز وي دو نؤت كير.

وي مؤئس وِل سپايرْل انتو فناز فليَم.
يو سيَ وير فرئنزيد فولز؟ وي دو نؤت كيَر.

ذه عالمز فِكُل لايك ذه برسات مَّنثس.
اِت سكوَرچز ذئن اِت كولز — وي دو نؤت كيَر.

ذه پث اڤ حق از فرؤت وِث خار و خون.
وي رئسْل ديَوز اند غولز — وي دو نؤت كيَر.

اُفّ! لئت ذئم لَف اند سيَ محزون هز جويند
اه حلقه اڤ بهلولز — وي دو نؤت كير!

Why Tease Me?

You say *bas, bas!*–but then say talk–why tease me?
You say sit, sit–and check the clock–why tease me?

I offer *guls*–you send back *masmūm* thorns.
You *ta'rīf* then you cruelly mock–why tease me?

The *ahl-i sū* have called me *siyah-post*.
If so then tread on me like *khāk*! Why tease me?

My house is made of glass but more so yours.
Don't act *hayrān* I threw that rock! Why tease me?

Mahzūn is no Ayyūb, still less Luqmān.
I lose my *sabr*–and you feign shock–why tease me?

Glossary

Mahzūn "The Saddened One." The poet's *takhallus*, i.e. pen name. It is customary to include the *takhallus* in the last couplet of a ghazal.
bas enough.
gul flower(s).
masmūm poisoned.
ta'rīf (offer a) compliment.

ahl-i sū bad company, bad friends.
siyah-post dark-skinned.
khāk soil, dust.
hayrān surprised, confused.
Ayyūb Job.
Luqmān a wise man mentioned in the Qur'an.
sabr patience.

واي تيزمي؟

يو سيَ بس بس! – بَت ذئن سيَ تؤك – واي تيز مي؟
يو سيَ سِت، سِت، سِت – اند چئك ذه كلؤك – واي تيز مي؟

آي اؤفر گُلز – اند يو سِئند بِك مسموم ثوَرنز.
يو تعريف ذئن يو كرولي مؤك – واي تيز مي؟

ذه اهل سو هڤ كؤلد مي سِيَه پوَست.
اِف سوَ ذئن ترئد اؤن مي لايك خاك! واي تيز مي؟

ماي هاوس اِز مِيد اڤ گُلَس بَت موَر سوَ يوَرز.
دوَنت اكت حيران آي ثرود ذلك رؤك! واي تيز مي؟

محزون اِز نوَ ايّوب، سْتِل لئس لقمان.
آي لوز ماي صبْر – اند يو فين شؤك – واي تيز مي؟

Me and You

Our eyes locked on the way to *namāz* in that sleepy *kū*.
You filled my heart to bursting like an *ārëzū* come true.
I sought you in the *sūq*, the *masjid*, and the *maykada*.
I searched until I knew: that you are me and I am you.

Glossary

namāz (Islamic) prayer, worship.
kū alleyway, street.
ārëzū wish, desire.
sūq market, marketplace.
masjid mosque.
maykada tavern.

مي اند يو

آر آيز لؤكت اؤن ذه ويَ تو نماز اِن ذَت سليپي كو.
يو فِلد ماي هارت تو بُرستنگ لايك ان آرَزو گُم ترو.
آي سؤت يو اِن ذه سوق، ذه مسجد، أند ذه مَيكده.
آي سَّرچت أنْتِل آي نيو: ذت يو آر مي أند آي أم يو.

Agar (If)

If I could wait, then wait I would.
Despite the decades' weight–I would.

If pride allowed me to bring low
My head at your high gate–I would.

You dared me to behead our love.
If you could bear my hate–I would.

If I could put out this *hirqat*
And know a cooler fate–I would.

If I, Mahzūn, could tame my soul
And find a tamer mate–I would.

Glossary

Mahzūn "The Saddened One."
The poet's *takhallus*, i.e. pen
name. It is customary to include
the *takhallus* in the last couplet
of a ghazal.
hirqat burn.

اگر (اِف)

آاِف آي كُد وَيت، ذئن وَيت آي وُد.
دِسپايت ذه دكيَدز وَيت – آي وَيت.

اف پرايد ألوَد مي تو بُرِنگ لوَ
ماي هئد أَت يوَر هاي گَيت – آي وُد.

يو دَيرد مي تو بِهئد آر لڤ.
اف يو كُد بيَر ماي هيَت – آي وُد.

اِف آي كُد پُت آوت دِس حرقت
اند نوَ اه كولر فيَت – آي وُد.

اِف آي، محزون، كُد تيم ما سوَل
آند فايند اه تيَمر ميَت – آي وُد.

Har Shab Manam Futāda
(Every Evening I Collapse)[2]

At every day's end I collapse at your *sarā*, my love.
The morning sun is witness to my ache and *āh*, my love.

Until my shattered bones become a fistful of dry dust
My anguished heart will always nourish our *hawā*, my love.

Our evening of *wisāl* did not survive the birth of dawn.
Woe unto me that I've become your *mubtalā*, my love.

Although I cannot bring my prideful self to kiss your feet
My soul is ever yours–I swear before *Khudā*, my love.

Come *jān-i jān*, bear witness to my *dilshikastagī*.
Can you not spare some favor for your *āshënā*, my love?

Pray cast a glance upon my wretched state with tender eyes.
You're *shāh-i husn* and Khusraw is your poor *gadā*, my love.

---

[2] Inspired by a Persian ghazal by Indo-Persian poet Amīr Khusraw
Dihlawī.

Glossary

har shab manam futāda P.
every evening I collapse.
sarā abode, house, palace.
āh expression of lament and
grief.
hawā desire, passion;
longing, attachment.
wisāl union with the lover.
mubtalā one afflicted (with
love or another ordeal.)

Khudā God.
jān-i jān soul of my soul, a
term of endearment.
dilshikastagī heartbreak.
āsh(ë)nā belovèd,
acquaintance, friend; adj.
familiar, acquainted.
shāh-i husn king of beauty.
gadā beggar; spiritual seeker.

هر شب منم فُتاده (ائثري ايثننگ آي گَلپس)

اَت ائثري ديَز ائند آي گَلپس ات يوَر سرا، ماي لَث.
ذه مَورننگ سَن اِز وتِنِس تو ماي ايَك اَند آه، ماي لَث.

اَنتِل ماي شَتَرد بوَنز بِگَم اه فِستفُل اف دراي دَست.
ماي آنگوشت هارت وِل اوَلويَز نَرِش آر هوا، ماي لَث.

آر ايثننگ اف وِصال دِد نوَت سَرثايث ذه بَرث اف دؤن.
وَ اَنتو مي ذت آيث بِگَم يوَر مُبتلا، ماي لَث.

اؤلذوَ آي گَنوَت برنگ ماي پرايدفُل سئلف تو كِس يوَر فيت.
ماي سوَل اِز ائثر يوَرز — آي سويَر بِفوَر خُدا، ماي لَث.

گَم جانِ جان، بيَر وِتِنِس تو ماي دِلشِكستگي.
گَن يو نوَت سپيَر سَم فيثر فوَر يوَر آشنا، ماي لَث.

پريَ گَست اه گَلَنس اَپؤن ماي رئچِد ستيَت وِث تئندر آيز.
يوَر شاهِ حُسن اَند خُسرَو اِز يوَر پور گدا، ماي لَث.

Marwa

My Marwa's fickle moods are *bēwafā*
Like sudden floods that ravage my *safā*.

One moment I might sip her sweet *mudām*.
The next I swallow *jāms* of cruel *jafā*.

When she departs she never glances back
While Mahzūn walks away *rū bar qafā*.

And when my *giryān* heart has had enough
I might exclaim, "*Ishqam! Amān! Kafā!*"

But then she smiles away the gloomy clouds
And I will whisper, "*ẓālimī ʿafā*."

Glossary

Mahzūn "The Saddened One." The poet's *takhallus*, i.e. pen name. It is customary to include the *takhallus* in the last couplet of a ghazal.
bēwafā treacherous, faithless.
safā peace of mind, tranquility.
mudām wine.
jām cup, glass.

jafā emotional cruelty or coldness.
rū bar qafā head turned backward.
giryān crying, weeping.
ishqam! amān! kafā my love! mercy! enough!
ẓālimī ʿafā my tyrant/oppressor has forgiven (me).

مروه

ماي مروَز فِكل مودز آر بيَوفا
لايك سَّدن فلدز ذت رَفِج ماي صِفا.

وَّن مؤمنت آي مايت سِپ هَّر سِويت مُدام
ذه نئكست آي سوؤلوَ جامز اف كرول جفا.

وئن شي دِپارتس شي نئثر گلَنسِز بك
وايل محزون وؤكس اويَّ رو بر قفا.

اند وئن ماي گريان هارت هَز هَد اِنَّف
آي ماي ائكسكليَّم "عِشقم! أمان! كفى!"

بَّت ذئن شي سمايلز اويَّ ذه گلومي كلاودز
اند آي وِل وِسپِر "ظالِمي عفا."

A Khusraw Ghazal[3]

My senses did not recognize that strange *manzil* that night
In every *kunj-u-sū* the people danced *bismil* that night.

A *parī-paykar, sarw-qadd, lāla-rukhsār, dilrubā*
From head to toe she was the hall's *āfat-i dil* that night.

The *raqīb*s reveled in your voice while, helpless, I
watched on.
My tongue was tied and well-formed speech became
mushkil that night.

It turned the bashful youth into a roving *rind*, that night.
And gentle-natured *āhū*s tore down their first kill, that night.

In *Lāmakān Khudāwand* headed that *majlis*, Khusraw.
Muhammad was the candlelight of our *mahfil* that night.

---

[3] Inspired by a Persian ghazal by Indo-Persian poet Amīr Khusraw
Dihlawī.

Glossary

manzil abode, stage.

kunj-u-sū corner and direction.

dance bismil dance like an animal being slaughtered, i.e. dance in a frenzy.

parī-paykar possessing a fairy-like form.

sarw-qadd cypress-statured.

lāla-rukhsār tulip-cheeked.

dilrubā stealer of hearts.

āfat-i dil affliction of the heart.

raqīb adversary, enemy.

mushkil difficult, problematic.

rind a dedicated Sufi who affects moral debauchery.

āhū gazelle.

Lāmakān "no-place," a divine realm beyond physicality.

Khudāwand Lord, God.

majlis assembly, congregation, meeting place.

mahfil assembly, congregation.

اہ خُسرو غزل

ماي سَئنسِز دِد نؤت رئگگنايز ذت ستريَنج منزل ذت نايت
ان ائثري كُنج و سو ذه پيپل دَنست بسمل ذت نايت.

اه پري پَيكر، سرْو قد، لاله رُخسار دِلرُبا
فرَم هئد تو تو شي وَز ذه هؤلز آفتِ دِل ذت نايت.

ذه رقيبز رئثلد اِن يور قويس وايل، هئلپلس، آي وؤچت اؤن.
ماي تَنگ وَز تايد اند وئل-فؤرمد سپيچ بِكيَم مُشكل ذَت نايت.

اِت تَرند ذه بَشفُل يوث اِنتو اه روَفنگ رِند، ذت نايت.
اند جئنتل-نيَچرد آهوز تؤر داون ذيَر فَرست كِل ذات نايت.

ان لامكان خُداوِند هئدِد ذت مجلس، خُسرو.
محمد وَز ذه كَندْل لايت اف آر محفل ذت نايت.

Khudā-yi Sūq (God of the Market)

A new *zamāna* flatly drones: the die is cast,
The Princes and the Powers are *bāzār-parast*.
"This world's a cage," thus knows the *mu'min*'s lonely heart,
"But look! I am a *markab* towards Allāh's *alast*."

Glossary

Khudā-yi Sūq God of the
Market.
zamāna epoch, era, Zeitgeist,
world.
bāzār-parast market-
worshipping.
mu'min believer, faithful.
markab ship, vessel, vehicle.

alast refers to the Qur'anic
covenant in Surah Al-A'raf
(7:172), where Allah asks souls,
alastu bi rabbikum ("Am I
not your Lord?") affirming
humanity's primordial
acknowledgment of divine
sovereignty.

خداي سوق

اه نو زمانه فلتلي درؤنز: ذه داي اِز گَست،
ذه پرِنسِز أند ذه پاورز آر بازارپرست.
"ذِس وًرلدز اه کيَج،" ذَس نوَز ذه مؤمنز لوَنلي هارت،
"بَّت لُك! آي ام اه مرکب توَردز اللهِز الست."

A Tribute to Rumi[4]

Listen to the *nay* and its *hikāyat*
And of apartness how it makes *shikāyat*.

It cries, "I was cut off from my *nay*-bed."
On hearing this, the people cried with dread.

I seek a breast that's torn up with *firāq*
To share my tale of pain and *ishtiyāq*.

For one who is dismembered from their *asl*
Will always long to reestablish *wasl*.

In every company I raised my *nāl*
A friend to those who suffered every *hāl*.

All based on their own *zann* became my *yār*
But no one meant to reach my core *asrār*.

From my lament my secret was not *dūr*
But eye and ear to know it lacked the *nūr*.

To *tan* and *jān* are *jān* and *tan manzūr*
But none may see the *jān* as per *dastūr*.

---

[4] This is a translation of the first ten verses of Rumi's famed *Mathnawī Ma'nawī*, a 25,000-verse Persian poem that is considered one the most important works of Islamic, and particularly Sufi, literature.

And since the *nay* sings fire, not mere wind
The fireless will scatter with the wind.

The fire of *ishq* is found inside the *nay*
The *jōsh* of *ishq* is found inside the *may*.

Glossary

nay (reed) flute.
hikāyat story.
shikāyat complaint.
firāq separation.
ishtiyāq longing.
asl origin.
wasl union with the belovèd.
nāl lament, complaint.
hāl state, status, condition, health.
zann conjecture, suspicion.
yār friend, companion, lover.

asrār plur. of *sirr* secret, mystery.
dūr far.
nūr light.
tan body, person.
jān soul, life-force, energy.
manzūr seen, visible.
dastūr permission, law, canon.
ishq (divine; extreme, all-consuming) love, passion.
jōsh boil, ardor, excitement.
may wine.

أه تْرِييوت تورومي

لِسن تو ذه نِي اند اتس حكايت
اند اف أپارتنس هاو اِت مَيكس شكايت.

اِت كرايز، "آي وَز گَت اؤف فرَم ماي نَي بئد."
اؤن هيرنگ ذس، ذه پيپل نالْد وِث درئد.

آي سيك اه برئست ذتس تورن أپ وث فِراق
تو شِيَر ماي تِيَل اف پين اند اشتياق.

فوَر وَن هو از دِسمئمبَّرد فرم ذيَر أصْل
وِل اؤلوِيَز لؤنگ تو ري-اِستَبْلِش وَصل.

اِن ائثري كمپني آي رِيزد ماي نال
اه فرئند تو ذوز هو سَفرد ائثري حال.

اؤل بِيَست اؤن ذيَر اؤن ظن بِكِيَم ماي يار
بَّت نوَ وَن مئنت تو ريچ ماي كوَّر أَسرار.

فرؤم ماي لُمئنت ماي سيكرت وؤز نؤت دور
بَّت آي اند اير تو نوَ اِت لَكت ذه نور.

تو تَن اند جان آر جان اند تَن مْنظور
بَّت نَن مِيَ سي ذه جان از پَّر دَستور.

اند سِنس ذه نَي سنگز فاير، نؤت مير وِند
ذه فايرلِس وِل سْكَتَّر وِث ذه وِند.

ذه فاير أَف عِشق اِز فاوند اِنسايد ذه نَي
ذه جوَش أَف عِشق اِز فاوند اِنسايد ذه مي.

Rumi Saves a Fruit Bandit

A hungry man perceived a tree
weighed down with fruit, and thought it free.
He climbed, and clambered, clawed, and clung,
got twigs in his face, and seeds in his lungs.
Until at last, he set his eyes
upon the fleshy, fruity prize.
And just as he stretched his fruit-thieving hand
a voice from below pierced his cochlea and
he looked down to earth for the very first time
since he had embarked on his hunger-fueled climb,
to see the land's *mālik* turned red-faced and mad
exclaiming invectives like "*ruswā*" and "cad"!
He ordered the climber's immediate descent
with overblown threats of vengeance half-meant.
Of course, our fruit-*duzd*, he gave no assent
so frightened he was of the old man's intent.
Their wont is well-known, when they are exposed:
wrong-doers will shirk the sanctions imposed.
But in his refusal, the *dirakht-naward*
paid little attention to pleasure or *dard*.
Chock-full of bravado, impudence he chose.
"This masculine oath I shall self-impose:
I'll never touch grass, nor will I be forced
for then I do swear, my wife is divorced!"
Perhaps from his father this vow he had learned
or from the fear-sickness that in him now burned.
Faced with this *tamāshā*, the mister below,

his rage and impatience continued to grow.
The dendrito-centric fracas reached the *muftī*
who learning the details, retorted, *chī guftī?!*
"Are we the high clerics, of turban and *jubba*
to only read *khutba*s and stare at the *qubba*?
So let us now hurry to counsel them both:
the bothered old man, and he of the oath."
He parleyed and pleaded in peasants' *patois*
and issued what seemed a balanced *fatwā*.
The *āqā* said no, the thief shall not pass
which made him more headstrong, that stranded *bēkas*
who languished three nights in foisted nirvana,
until a *pīr* said, consult with Mawlānā!
The most revered Rūmī declared, "I'm amazed
how some of our folks' behavior seems crazed!
Now say to the climber, jump onto a raised
tree trunk that's adjacent, and Allāh be praised!
Then simply descend right onto a horse
and touch not the ground through perjury or force!"
I'll leave it to you, my dear *sāmi'īn*
to locate the moral; my own I shall glean:
Medieval folks loved their saints multi-use
to deal with all issues, both plain and obtuse.
Like having at hand a loophole tutorial
on how to untangle dilemmas arboreal.

Glossary

mālik land-owner, landlord.

ruswā disgraced, ignominious.

duzd thief.

dirakht-naward tree-climber.

dard pain.

tamāshā spectacle, show.

muftī Muslim legal expert.

chī guftī? P. what did you say?

jubba an outer robe, with full sleeves and long skirts, and open in front.

khutba sermon.

qubba (mosque) dome.

fatwā (religion) legal opinion.

āqā mister, master, lord.

bēkas lacking a companion, lonely, friendless.

pīr old man; religious guide or master, a saint.

sāmi'īn listeners, audience.

رومي سيَقزاه فروت بَندِت

اه هنگري مَن پُرسيقد اه تري
ويَد داون وث فروت، اند ثؤت اِت فري.
هي كلايمد، اند كلمرد، كلؤد، اند كلَنگ،
گؤت تُوگز ان هز فيَس، اند سيدز ان هز لَنگز.
أنتِل ات لَست، هي سئت هز آيز
أپؤن ذه فلئشي، فروتي پرايز.
اند جَست از هي سترئچت هِز فروت-ثيقنگ هند
اه قويس فرَم بِلوَ پيرست هِز كؤكليه لند
هي لُكت داون تو أرث فوَر ذه قئري فَرست تايم
سِنس هي هد اِمباركت اؤن هِز هَنگر فيولد كلايم،
تو سي ذه لَندز مالك تُرند رئد-فيَست اند مد
اِكسكليَمنگ اِنقئكتِقز لايك "رُسوا" اند "كد"!
هي اوَردرد ذه كلايمرز اِميدييت دِسئنت
وِث اوَقربلوَن ثرئتس اق قئنجنس هَف مئنت.
اق كوَرس، آر فروت-دُزد، هي گيَق نوَ أسئنت
سوَ فرايتند هي وَز اق ذه اوَلد منز اِنتئنت.
ذيَر ووُنت از وئل نوَن، وئن ذيَ آر اِكسپوَزد:
رؤنگ دووَرز وِل شُرك ذه سَنكشنز اِمپوَزد.
بَت ان هِز رِفيوزَل، ذه دِرخت نَوَرد
پيَد لِتل اتئنشن تو پلئثَر اور دَرد.
چوَك-فُل اق برَقادوَ، اِمپيودنس هي چوَز.
"دِس مَسْكلن اوَث آي شَل سئلف-اِمپوَز:
آيل نئثر تَچ گرس، نوَر وِل آي بي فوَرست
فوَر ذئن آي دو سُويَر، ماي وايف اِز دِقوَرست!"
پَرهَپس فرَم هِز فاذر دِس قاو هي هَد لُرند
اوَر فرَم ذه فير-سِكنس ذَت اِن هِم ناو بَرند.

فِيَست وِث ذس تماشا، ذه مِتسر بِلوَ،
هِز رِيَج اند اِمپيَشِنس گَنتِنيود تو گروَ.
ذه دِئندِرتوَ-سِئنترك فراكا رِيچت ذه مُفتي
هو لُرننگ ذه ديتيَلز، رِتوَرتِد، چي گُفتى؟!
”آز وِي ذه هاي كلئِركس، اڤ تَّربِن اند جُبّه
تو اوَنلي رِيد خُطبَز اند ستيَر ات ذه قبّه؟
سوَ لئِت أَس ناو هَّري تو كاونسل ذئم بوَث:
ذه بِؤذرد اوَلد من، اند هي اڤ ذه اوَث.“
هي پارليد اند پليدِد ان پئزنتس پاتوا
اند اِشود وَّت سيمد اه بَلنِست فتوى.
ذه آقا سئد نوَ، ذه ثيف شَل نؤت پس
وِچ ميَد هم موَر هئدستروَّنگ، ذت سُتْرَندِد
هو لَنگوِشت ثري نايتس اِن فويستِد نِرڤانه،
أَنتِل اه پير سئد، گَنسِّلت وِث مَولانا!
ذه موَست رِڤيرد رومي دِكلِيَرد، ”آيم أَميَزد
هاو سَّم اڤ آر فوَكس بِهيَڤر سيمز كرِيَزد!
ناو سيَ تو ذه كلايمر، جَّمپ اؤنتو اه رِيَزد
تري ترِّئنك ذَتس اجيَسنت، اند الله بي پرِيَزد!
ذئن سِمپلي دِسئند رايت اؤنتو اه هوَرس
اند تَّج نؤت ذه گراوند ثرو پرجري اوَر فوَرس!“
آيل ليڤ اِت تو يو، ماي دير سامعين
تو لوَكيَت ذه موَرل؛ ماي اوَن آي شَل گلين:
مِديڤل فوَكس لُقد ذيَر سيَنتس مَّلتي-يوس
تو ديل وِث اؤل اِشوز، بوَث پلِيَن اند اؤبتوس
لايك هڤنگ أَت هند اه لوِهوَل تُتوَريَّل
اؤن هاو تو أَنتَنگل دايلئمَّز آربوَريَّل.

A Tribute to Amīr Khusraw[5]

I am an *ishq-bāwar*; I have no need of rites and *rasm*.
My sinews are in knots; I gird with no *zunnār* at all.

Away from my *bālīn*, you *ghāfil* and naïve *tabīb*!
How can an *āshiq* heal from *ishq* with no *dīdār* at all?

If there be not a *nākhudā* to guide our seeking ship
We have *Khudā*; a *nākhudā* is not *darkār* at all.

The *khalq* accuse Khusraw of practicing *but-parastī*.
Ārē! Ārē! I follow not the *khalq*'s *raftār* at all!

Glossary

ishq-bāwar a believer in divine love, passion.

rasm custom, tradition; drawing.

zunnār a waist-belt formerly worn by Zoroastrians or Christians.

bālīn bed(ding).

ghāfil thoughtless, inattentive.

tabīb physician, doctor.

āshiq lover, person afflicted with *ishq*.

ishq (divine; extreme, all-consuming) love, passion.

dīdār visitation, seeing the belovèd.

nākhudā sea-captain, skipper.

Khudā God.

darkār necessary.

khalq people, society, masses; created beings, creatura.

but-parastī idol-worship, paganism.

ārē yes, truly, indeed.

raftār behavior, manner; way.

---

[5] Inspired by a Persian ghazal by Indo-Persian poet Amīr Khusraw Dihlawī.

اه تُربِيوت تو امير خُسرَو

آي ام ان عِشقباوَر؛ آي هڤ نوَ نيد اڤ رايت اند رَسم.
ماي سِنيوز آر اِن نؤتس؛ آي گِّرد وث نوَ زُنّار ات اؤل.

اويَ فرَّم ماي بالين، يو غافل اند نايِيڤ طبيب!
هاو گَن ان عاشق هيل فرَّم عِشق وِث نوَ ديدار ات اؤل؟

اِف ذيَر بي نؤت أه ناخُدا تو گايد آر سيكِنگ شِپ
وي هڤ خُدا؛ اه ناخدا اِز نؤت دركار ات اؤل.

ذه خَلق اكيوز خُسرَو اڤ پركتسنگ بُتپِرستي.
آريَ! آريَ! آي ڤؤلو نؤت ذه خلقِس رفتار اَت اؤل!

Tourists' Friend

The local-passing Mehmandoost
whose *nom d'artiste* means traveler's friend:
among the guides, he ruled the roost
and spun tall stories without end.

"Because I speak ten tongues and one
I aid the *wālī* without fail."
At first the yarns were harmless fun
until he dropped this iffy tale.

He claimed, "No other guide can speak
the English tongue in Isfahān.
No other fixer jokes in Greek
or charms the girls in Catalan!

"But Arabic–when have I lied?
is new to my linguistic brain!"
I said, "*akhī*, that claim's belied
by your perfection of the ʿ*ayn*.

"Your idiom's clear, your verbs ring true.
I must declare your speech is native.
I won't, however, breathe a clue
as your persona's quite creative."

I do not blame sir Mehmandoost
that Arab guide in Isfahān.
He changed his name to get a boost
you'd surely do the same, *dōstān*.

Glossary

wālī governor, prefect.
akhī my brother.
ʿ*ayn* a voiced pharyngeal
fricative in Arabic that is
difficult for non-native speakers
to pronounce.
dōstān friends.

تورسـتس فرئند

ذه لوكل-پَسنگ مهماندوست
هوز نوم دارتيست ميز ترَقُلرز فرئند:
اَمَنگ ذه گايدز، هي رولد ذه روست
اند سپَّن تؤل ستوريز وِذاوت ائند.

"بِگَز آي سپيك تئن تَنگز اَند وَن
آي اَيَد ذه والي وذاوت فيَّل."
ات فَرست ذه يارنز وَر هارملس فَن
اَنتل هي درؤپت ذِس اِڧي تيل.

هي كلَيمد، "نوَ اذر گايد كَن سپيك
ذه انگلش تَنگ ان اصفهان.
نوَ اذر فِكس ر جوَكس ان گريك
اوَر چارمز ذه گرلز اِن گَتَّلَن!

"بُت عربك – وئن هڤ آي لايد؟ –
از نو تو ماي لِنگوِستِك برِيَن!"
آي سئد، "أخي، ذت كلَيمز بِلايد
باي يور پَّرفِئكشن اڤ ذه عين.

"يور اِدِيَمز كلير، يور قُربز رنگ ترو.
آي مَست دِكلِير يور سپيچ از نِيَتِڤ.
آي ووَنت، هاوئڤر، بريذ اه كلو
از يور پَّرسوَنَز كوايت كرِيَتِڤ."

آي دو نؤت بليَم سَر مهماندوست
ذت عرب گايد ان اصفهان.
هي چيَنجد هِز نيم تو گئت اه بوست
يود شُرلي دو ذه سيَم، دوستان.

My *Rashk-i Qamar*

My *rashk-i qamar*
Your lips are *shakar*
Your brows full of *nāz*.

You snared my *nazar*
I'm sick with *kadar*
Amān ay dilbāz!

Glossary

rashk-i qamar envy of the moon, i.e. beautiful belovèd.
shakar sugar.
nāz coquetry.
nazar eyesight, (field of) vision; appearance; opinion.
kadar sadness, sorrow, anxiety.

amān an interjection conveying strong emotions like yearning or pleading.
ay oh.
dilbāz lover who plays with hearts.

ماي رَشكِ قمر

ماي رَشكِ قَمَر
يوَر لپِس آر شَگَر
يوَر براوز فُل اڤ ناز.

يو سنيَرد ماي نظر
آيم سك وث كدر
امان آي دِلباز!

Ghazal on an Empty Stomach

I'm craving some *kabāb* tonight
with Laylā and Rabāb tonight.

I've saved my *muzd* for several weeks.
The *duzds* have much to rob tonight.

This hungry pauper yearns to eat
like Jasha'-ville's *nawwāb* tonight.

Unless I get my *murgh* and *nān*
I shall break down and sob tonight.

The bard who dined with fat *wazīrs*
shall join the *qabā* mob tonight.

Glossary

kabāb meat in pieces and roasted on skewers.
muzd wages.
duzd thief.
Jasha'-ville "Gluttonville." A very real town.
nawwāb ruler, governor, lord.

murgh bird; chicken.
nān bread, especially the type baked in Iran and Persianate cultures; food.
wazīr viziers, minister, high government official.
qabā coarse, vulgar.

غزل اؤن أَن ائمپتي ستَّمَك

آيم كريَثفنگ سَم كباب تُنيات
وِث ليلى اند رِباب تُنايت.

آيڤ سيَقد ماي مُزد فوَر سئقرل ويكس
ذه دُزدز هَڤ مَج تو رؤب تُنايت.

ذِس هنگري پؤپر يَرنز تو ايت
لايك جشعقِلز نواب تُنايت.

أَنلئس آي گئت ماي مُرغ اند نان
آي شَل بريَك داون اند سؤب تُنايت.

ذه بارد هو دايند وِث فت وزيرز
شَل جوين ذه قبا مؤد تُنايت.

Yūsuf

A spurned *payghāmbar* fled and disappeared.
The ingrates ate God's bread and disappeared.

Young Yūsuf's still confined within his well.
Two crows pecked at his head and disappeared.

The *ghayr*s cheered on my *āshnā*'s wily ways
Who left my *qalb* for dead and disappeared.

I keep my *shawq* beside my night *firāsh*
For her who scorched my bed and disappeared.

If—as they claim—Mahzūn is *khud-parast*
Why then has he not fled and disappeared?

Glossary

Mahzūn "The Saddened One."
The poet's *takhallus*, i.e. pen
name. It is customary to include
the *takhallus* in the last couplet
of a ghazal.
payghāmbar messenger, prophet.
Yūsuf the prophet Joseph.
ghayr another person; rival,
enemy.

āshnā lover; companion;
acquaintance.
qalb heart, core, inner life.
shawq yearning, longing.
firāsh mattress, couch, bedding.
khud-parast self-worshipping.

يوسُف

اه سپرند پيغامبر فلئد اند دسپيرد.
ذه انگريتس ايت گؤدز برئد اَند دسَّپيرد.

ينگ يوسُفس ستل كنفايند وذن هز وئل.
تو كرۆز پِكت ات هِز هئد اَند دِسَّپيرد.

ذه غَيرز چيرد اؤن ماي آشناز وايلي وێز
ذت لئفت ماي قلب فوٚر دئد فوَّر اَند دِسَّپيرد.

آي كيپ ماي شَوق بِسايد ماي نايت فِراش
فوَّر هَّر هو سكوَّرچت ماي بئد اَند دِسَّپيرد.

اِف ــ از ذيّ كليم ــ محزون از خودپرست
واي ذئن هَز هي نؤت فلئد اَند دِسَّپيرد؟

Bār-i Wujūd (The Burden of Being)

My *jān* is quartered by the strain of being.
What *wirtha* have I save the pain of being?

Would that I could unite with heaven's host
Who worships God throughout this reign of being.

A *bashar*'s life: a few crushed seeds and *khāk*.
Silenus warned against the bane of being.

The world is heedless yet our *khātir* weeps
For those who never walked the lane of being.

Though old Mahzūn might change his dress and speech
No *burda* hides the lasting stain of being.

Glossary

Mahzūn "The Saddened One." The poet's *takhallus*, i.e. pen name. It is customary to include the *takhallus* in the last couplet of a ghazal.

jān soul, life-force, energy.

wirth(a) inheritance, heritage.

bashar human (being), mankind.

khāk dust.

khātir cogitation, thinking, remembrance.

burda cloak, mantle.

بارِوُجود (ذه بُردن اف بيينگ)

ماي جان از كؤرترد باي ذه سترين اف بيينگ.
وَت وِرثه هف آي سيَف ذه پَين اف بيينگ؟

وُد ذت آي كُد يُنايت وث هئثنز هوَست
هو وَرشِپ گؤد ثروآوت ذس رِين اف بيينگ؟

اه بشرز لايف: اه فيو كرَشت سيدز اند خاك.
سايلينس وَرند اگئنست ذه بِين اف بيينگ.

ذه وَرلد از هيدلئس يئت آر خاطر ويِس
فؤر ذوَز هو نئثر وؤكت ذه لَين اف بيينگ.

ذوَ اوَلد محزون مايت چيَنج هِز درئس اند سپيچ
نوَ بُرده هايدز ذه لَستنگ ستين اف بيينگ.

My Lovely Fahmīda

My lovely Fahmīda
Your *sharm* broke my *dīda*
In Friday's *bāzār*.

This life is *sanjīda*
Why make it *pēchīda*
Why kindle the *nār*?

My *rūh* is *ranjīda*
My *jān* is *nālīda*
And will is *bēkār!*

Glossary

sharm shame, modesty.
dīda eye, vision, sight.
bāzār (open air) market, bazaar.
sanjīda serious, grave.
pēchīda complicated, twisted.
nār (hell) fire.

rūh spirit, soul.
ranjīda grieved, afflicted.
jān soul, life-force, energy.
nālīda lamenting, weeping.
bēkār useless, worthless, helpless.

ماي لَقْلي فهميده

ماي لَقْلي فهميده
يۆر شرم بروَك ماي ديده
اِن فرايديز بازار.

ذِس لايف اِز سنجيده
واي ميَك اِت پيَچيده
واي كِندل ذه نار؟

ماي روح اِز رنجيده
ماي جان اِز ناليده
اند وِل اِز بيَكار!

Pied *Nayzan* (Piper)

He blew sweet *nafas* in his *nay*
As we imbibed his heady *may.*
And now this *sāda, zāhid* man
Would rather dance to *daff* than pray.

Glossary

nayzan piper, flautist.
nafas breath; soul, life.
nay (reed) flute.
may wine.

sāda simple, naïve.
zāhid devout, ascetic,
renouncing worldly concerns.
daff frame drum.

پايد نيَزَن (پايپر)

هي بلو سويت نفس ان هز نَي
از وي امبايبْد هز هئدي مي.
اند ناو ذس ساده، زاهد من
وُد رَذر دنس تو دف ذن پريَ.

Bād-i Sabā (The East Wind)

I nursed my wounded *āberū*
But still my *dil* was *tang* for you.

I thought my *yār* was ever true.
My simple *fitrat* had no clue.

When *bād-i sabā* blows anew
I smell again your sweet *khushbū*.

Glossary

bād-i sabā morning or east wind, zephyr, refreshing breeze.
āberū honor, reputation, lit. "water of the face."
dil heart.
tang tight, constrained; longing, yearning.

yār friend, companion, lover.
fitrat innate human nature.
khushbū n.adj. fragrant, sweet smelling; fragrance.

بادِ صبا (ذه ايست وِند)

آي نَرست ماي ووندِد آبِرو
بَّت سُتِل ماي دِل وَز تَنگ فوَر يو.

آي ثؤت ماي يار وَز ائثر ترو.
ماي سمپل فطرت هَد نوَ كلو.

وئن بادِ صبا بلوَز انو
آي سمئل اگئن يور سوِت خُوشبو.

She'd Had Enough

Your *qadd* was tall, your cheeks were pink.
Your *zulfs* as dark as Baghdād ink.

You lay in wait upon my path.
Full lips aflame with *qirmiz* wrath.

And being *mast-u-ghamzada*
I said, good night, oh *maykada*.

A drear monsoon had struck that *shām*.
I did not see you spring your *dām*.

Though drenched in rain, you stayed well-bred.
And hurled no curse, but glared instead.

I swore an oath to mend my way
But *hayf ay hayf*! You did not stay!

I only have myself to blame,
Who sold *wisāl* for *ranj* and shame.

Glossary

qadd height, stature, poise.
zulf (hair) curl, tress.
qirmiz crimson in color.
must-u-ghamzada drunk
and afflicted by sadness and
melancholy.
maykada tavern, pub, wine
cellar.

shām eve(ning).
dām trap, net, snare; price.
hayf ay hayf what a pity!
wisāl union with the belovèd.
ranj suffering, affliction.

شيد هَد اِنَف

يوَر قد وَز تؤل، يوَر چيكس وَر پِنك.
يوَر زُلفس از دارك از بغداد اِنك.

يو ليَ اِن ويَت اپوَن ماي پِث.
فل لِپس افليَم وِث قِرمِز رَث.

اند بيينگ مَست و غمزده.
آي سئد، گُد نايت، اوَ مَيكَدَه.

اه درير مؤنسون هَد سِتْرِك ذت شام.
آي دِد نؤت سي يو سِپْرِنگ يوَر دام.

ذوَ درئنچت اِن رِنَن، يو ستيَد وئل-برئد.
آند هَرلد نوَ گَرس، بَت گليَرد اِنْستئد.

آي سوقَر ان اوَث تو مئند ماي ويَ
بت حيف أي حيف! يو دِد نؤت ستيَ!

آي اوَنلي هڤ مايسئلف تو بليَم،
هو سوَلد وِصال فوَر رنج اند شام.

114

Dū Jahān (The Two Worlds)

They say there are two *ālam*s but I've only known the one.
I am an *akmah* who cannot perceive the brilliant sun.
Ah well, perhaps my seemingly pure *nīyāt* will suffice!
For God will call us anyway–when all is said and done.

Glossary

dū two.
jahān world.
ālam world.
akmah a person born blind.
nīyāt intention.

دو جهان (ذَه تو وَرلْدز)

ذيَ سيَ ذير آر تو عالمز بَّت آيِف اوَنلي نوَن ذه وَن.

آي ام ان اكمه هو گنؤت پُرسيف ذه بُرِليَّنت سَّن.

آه وئل، پُرهپس ماي سيمنگلي پيور نيّت وِل سَّفايس!

فوَر گؤد وِل كؤل أس ائنيوَيّ — وين اؤل اِز سئد اند دَن.

Dam ū Ashk (Breaths and Tears)

With every sigh, a *dam* of pain.
My lungs inhale the *gham* of pain.

Last night I stumbled upon Mass.
I saw an *āshiq* Lamb of pain.

Hakīms can offer no *darmān*
To *dils* that drink the *sam* of pain.

My weeping filled a *bahr-i āh.*
Each *dam'a* cries, "I am of pain."

The *parīs* play until they drown.
They breached Iskandar's dam of pain.

"You shall wait long for love, Mahzūn"
Thus spoke my *jām-i jam* of pain.

Glossary

Mahzūn "The Saddened One." The poet's *takhallus*, i.e. pen name. It is customary to include the *takhallus* in the last couplet of a ghazal.

dam breath; moment, instant; blood.

ashk tear (from eye).

dam'a tear (from eye).

gham grief, sorrow, chagrin.

āshiq lover, person afflicted with *ishq*.

hakīm doctor, physician; sage.

darmān remedy, cure.

dil heart.

bahr-i āh sea of lament.

parī fairy, fay, nymph.

Iskandar Alexander the Macedonian.

jām-i jam a mythical cup used by ancient Persian kings to see the future.

دَم و اشك (برئث اند تيرز)

وِث ائثري سـاي، اه دَم اڤ پيَن.
ماي لَـنگز اِنهيَل ذه غَم اڤ پيَن.

لَست نايت آي سْتَّبلد أپؤن مَس.
آي سؤ ان عاشق لَم اڤ پيَن.

حكيمز كان اؤفر نوَ درمان
تو دِلز ذت درِنك ذه سم اڤ پيَن.

ماي ويپنگ فِلد اه بَحرِ آه.
ايچ دَمعه كرايز، "آي ام اڤ پيَن."

ذه پريز پليَ أَنتِل ذيَ دراون.
ذيَ بريچت اِسكندرز دم اڤ پيَن.

"يو شل ويَت لؤنگ فوَر لڤ، محزون"
ذَس سپؤك ماي جامِ جم اڤ پيَن.

Our Drinks–A Ghazal

There's nothing like black *chāy* to land a meal.
The *istikāna*s clink and sound divine.

Then add some spice and milk for *karak* tea.
A tasty, thundery drink that hits divine.

They say that *qahwa* used to be mulled wine.
Now coffee's black as ink and smells divine.

It contrasts with the white of sharp *laban*.
The bubbles rise, then sink, then pop: divine.

Laban is cousin to the Turks' *ayran*.
So tart it makes you blink and blurt, "divine!"

The rogues of Araby pressed fiery dates.
It brought them to the brink and felt divine.

Old *rind*s partook of *bāda* from Shīrāz.
The drinker would not think–just wax divine.

Small children love the essence of the rose.
It renders milk dark-pink and looks divine.

The juicy sacrifice of plump *rummān*
Can make your worries shrink by will divine.

Some say that guilt adds zing to splendid drinks.
Who knew indulgent sin could taste divine?

Glossary

chāy tea.

istikāna small glass used for tea.

karak a type of spiced milk tea, from the Urdu کڑک (kaṛak, "bolt of thunder"), therefore referred to as 'thundery.'

qahwa coffee; historically, mulled wine.

laban a type of dairy drink based on yoghurt, popular in the Arab World.

ayran a drink similar to Arabic *laban*, popular in Turkey.

rind a dedicated Sufi who affects moral debauchery.

bāda wine.

rummān pomegranate.

آور دُرنكس – اَه غَزَل

ذيرز نَئثنگ لايك بُلك چاي تو لَند اه ميل.
ذه اِستكائز گُلِنك أند ساوند دِثاين.

ذئن اد سَم سپايس اند مِلك فوَر كرك تي.
اه تيَستي، ئُندري درِنك ذت هِتس دِثاين.

ذيَ سيَ ذت قهوه يوسد تو بي مَلد واين.
ناو كؤفيز بُلك أز اِنك اند سمئلز دِثاين.

اِت كؤنترَستس وِث ذه وايت أف شارپ لَبَن.
ذه بُبلز رايز، ذئن سِنك، ذئن پؤپ – دِثاين.

لبَن از گَزن تو ذه تُركس آيران.
سوَ تارت اِت ميَكس يو بُلِنك أند بلُرت، "دِثاين!"

ذه روَگز اف عَرَبي پرئست فايري ديَتس.
اِت برؤت ذئم تو ذه بُرنك أند فئلت دِثاين.

اوَلد رِندز پارتُك اف باده فرَم شيراز.
ذه دُرِنكر وُد نؤت ثِنك – جَست وَكس دِثاين.

سمؤل چِلدرن لَف ذه ائسِنس اف ذه روَز.
اِت رئندَّرز مِلك دارك-پِنك أند لُكس دِثاين.

ذه جوسي سكرِفايس اف پْلَمپ رُمّان
گَن مێك يوَر وَريز شْرِنك باي وِل دِڤاين.

سَم سي ذت گِلت أدز زنگ تو سپلئنڊِد درِنكس.
هو نو اِندَّلجنت سِن كُد تێست دِڤاين؟

A Ghazal

This *shaydā* is in pain tonight.
For he expects no gain tonight.

Our tryst last week was but a fluke.
I know you shall abstain tonight.

The fire of *ishq* will surely drive
This pious man insane tonight.

Alone I launched my *kārawān*.
But others joined my lane tonight.

"Mahzūn's *majnūn*," the gossips said.
He's weeping with the rain tonight.

Glossary

Mahzūn "The Saddened One." The poet's *takhallus*, i.e. pen name. It is customary to include the *takhallus* in the last couplet of a ghazal.
shaydā maddened by love.
ishq (divine; extreme, all-consuming) love, passion.
kārawān caravan, body of travelers.
majnūn crazy, insane, Jinn-possessed.

اه غزل

ذس شيدا اِز اِن پيَن تُنايت.
فوَر هي اِكسپئكتس نوَ گيَن تُنايت.

آر تُرِست لَست ويك وَز بَت اه فلوك.
آي نوَ يو شَل أبستيَن تُنايت.

ذه فاير اُف عشق وِل شُرلي درايڤ
ذِس پايس من اِنسيَن تُنايت.

الوَن آي لؤنتچت ماي كاروان.
بَت أذرز جويند ماي ليَن تُنايت.

"محزونز مجنون"، ذه گؤسِپس سئد.
هيز ويپينگ وِث ذه ريَن تُنايت.

Gham (Sorrow)

I hid my hermit's shame with *gham*.
The *sāqī* pairs my name with *gham*.

The *qaws* is grey, the leaves are dry.
My seasons taste the same with *gham*.

I used to strut with rakish pride.
But now my gait is lame with *gham*.

This raucous *shātir* rocked the town—
His *tanz* is rendered tame with *gham*.

Young revelers come with fun and *mul*.
Except Mahzūn who came with *gham*.

Glossary

Mahzūn "The Saddened One." *sāqī* cup-bearer.
The poet's *takhallus*, i.e. pen *qaws* rainbow.
name. It is customary to include *shātir* clever, sly; thief, conman.
the *takhallus* in the last couplet *tanz* banter, ridicule.
of a ghazal. *mul* wine.

gham grief, sorrow, chagrin.

غم (سؤرق)

آي هِد ماي هًرمِتس شيَم وِث غم.
ذه ساقي پيَرز ماي نيَم وِث غم.

ذه قَوس اِز گريَ، ذه ليڤز آر دراي.
ماي سيزْنز تيَست ذه سيَم وِث غم.

آي يوستُ ستْرَت وِث ريَكِش پرايد.
بًت ناو ماي گيَت اِز ليم وِث غم.

ذِس رؤكس شاطِر رؤكت ذه تاون —
هِز طنْز اِز رئندرد تيَم وِث غم.

يَنگ رئثلًرز گم وِث فًن آند مل.
اِكْسئپت محزون هو كيَم وِث غم.

He Slew Me With a Wink[6]

He[7] slew me with a wink and framed *qazā* as his *bahāna*.
Then turned his eyes away and claimed *hayā* as his *bahāna*.

He touched another's shoulder out of pure *lutf-u-karam*.
But when he saw my face, "my foot slipped, ah!" was his *bahāna*.

I headed to the mosque in hope of glimpsing his sweet face.
He took his *rukh* in hand and read *du'ā* as his *bahāna*.

He graced the *kūcha* when he heard my *āwāz* calling out.
"I'm simply giving alms to some *gadā*," was his *bahāna*.

How can the *zāhid* bear the *parīrukh*'s pristine *jamāl*.
Inside his cell he claimed to fear *Khudā* as his *bahāna*.

Glossary

qazā fate, predestination.

bahāna excuse, pretext.

hayā diffidence, modesty.

lutf-u-karam kindness and favor.

rukh cheek; face.

du'ā prayer, supplication.

kūcha alley, lane.

āwāz voice.

gadā beggar; spiritual seeker.

zāhid hermit.

parīrukh angel-faced, fairy-faced.

jamāl beauty.

Khudā God.

---

6 Inspired by a Persian ghazal by Qatīl Lāhōrī.

7 Although the Persian third person singular pronoun is gender-unmarked, the original poem seems to have been addressed to a male.

هي سلو مي وِث اه وِنك

هي سلو مي وِث اه وِنك اند فرِيمد قضا اَز هِز بِهانه.
ذئن تَّرند هِز آيز اوِيَ اند كلِيَمد حيا اَز هِز بِهانه.

هي تَّچت اَنَّدرز شَوَلدر آوت اف بيور لُطف و كرم.
بَّت وئن هي سؤ ماي فيَس، "ماي فُت سْلِپت، آه!" وَز هِز بِهانه.

آي هئدِد تو ذه مؤسك اِن هوَپ اف گُلِمپِسنگ هِز سويت فيَس.
هي تُك هِز رُخ ان هند اَند ريد دُعا اَز هِز بِهانه.

هي گرِنست ذه كوچه وئن هي هَّرد ماي آواز كؤلنگ آوت.
"آيم سِمپلي گِثِنگ آلمز تو سَّم گدا"، وَز هِز بِهانه.

هاو گَن ذه زاهد بير ذه پري رُخس پُرِستين جمال.
اِنسايد هِز سئل هي كلِيَمد تو فير خُدا اَز هِز بِهانه.

Ahmaq-i Jadīd (Modern Fool)

Condemned to tame the *azhdahā*
And glean some remnants of *bahā;*

To rummage through his ruined *kanz*
For wisdom veiled as Bahlūl's *tanz;*

And recreate in fleeing words
The *mantiq* of the searching birds.

The lot of *ahmaq-i jadīd:*
To be both *murshid* and *murīd,*

And resurrect in lonesome mind
The souls our forebears left behind.

Glossary

ahmaq-i jadīd modern fool.

azhdahā dragon, serpent.

bahā splendor, beauty, glory.

kanz treasure.

Bahlūl epithet of Abū Wahab ibn ʿAmr, a historical figure who feigned madness in order to speak truth to power.

tanz satire, mockery.

mantiq reasoning, logic. A reference to Attār's Mantiq at-Tayr, *Conference of the Birds.*

murshid guide.

murīd disciple, student.

احمقِ جديد (مؤدرن فول)

گَندئمد تو تیَم ذه اژدها
اند گلین سَم رئمننتس اڤ بها؛

تو رَمج ثرو هِز روپند گَنز
فوَر وِزدَم ڤیَلد از بهلولز طَنز؛

اند رِبکریَت اِن فلیینگ وردز
ذه مَنطِق اڤ ذه سَرچنگ بردز.

ذه لؤت اڤ احمقِ جديد:
تو بي بوَث مُرشد آند مُرید،

آند رئزرئکت اِن لوَنسَّم مايند
ذه سوَلز آر فوَربیَرز لئفت بهايند.

Glossary

ab [اب] father.

abd [عبد] slave, servant, human being.

ābërū [آبرو] honor, reputation, lit. "water of the face."

abyāt [ابيات] plur. of *bayt* [بيت] verse, line of poetry.

āfat-i dil [آفتِ دل] affliction of the heart.

afsāna [افسانه] fairy tales, stories.

afsōs [افسوس] sadness, distress; woe is me! pity!

agarna [اگرنه] otherwise.

āh [آه] ah! an expression of lament, sadness, or pain.

ahl-i sū [اهلِ سو] bad company, bad friends.

ahmaq [احمق] fool(ish), stupid, rash.

ahmaq-i jadīd [احمقِ جديد] modern fool.

āhū [آهو] gazelle.

ahwāl [أحوال] circumstances, conditions.

ajnabī [اجنبي] foreigner, stranger.

akhbār [اخبار] information, news, gossip.

akhī [اخي] my brother.

akmah [اكمه] a person born blind.

ālam [عالم] (material) world.

alast [الست] refers to the Qur'anic covenant in Surah Al-A'raf (7:172), where Allah asks souls, *alastu bi rabbikum* [ألستُ بربكم؟] ("Am I not your Lord?") affirming humanity›s primordial acknowledgment of divine sovereignty.

ālim [عالِم] scholar, savant.

ālūda [آلوده] stained, polluted.

amān [امان] an interjection conveying strong emotions like yearning or pleading; mercy!

ān [آن] period of time; present moment.

āqā [آقا] mister, master, lord.

aql [عقل] mind, reason, intellect.

arbāb [ارباب] master, archon (in the Gnostic sense).

ārē [آری] yes, truly, indeed.

ārëzū [آرزو] wish, desire.

ārif [عارف] gnostic, knower of spiritual or mystical truths.

āsh(ë)nā [آشنا] love, acquaintance, friend; adj. familiar, acquainted.

āshiq [عاشق] (passionate) lover.

ashk [اشك] tear (from eyes).

āshnā [آشنا] lover; companion; acquaintance.

asl [اصل] origin.

asrār [اسرار] plur. of *sirr* [سر] secret, mystery.

ātish [آتش] fire.

āwāz [آواز] voice.

awrāq-i khizān-dīda [اوراق خزاندیده] autumn-withered pages/ leaves.

ay kāsh [اي كاش] I wish.

ʿayn [عین] a voiced pharyngeal fricative in Arabic that is difficult for non-native speakers to pronounce.

ayran [آیران] a similar drink to Arabic *laban*, popular in Turkey.

ayyār [عیّار] vagabond, knave.

Ayyūb [ایوب] Job.

azhdahā [اژدها] dragon, serpent.

azm [عزم] will, determination.

bāda [باده] wine.

badan [بدن] body.

bad-hālān [بدحالان] miserable people.

bād-i sabā [بادِ صبا] morning or east wind, zephyr, refreshing breeze.

bāghbān [باغبان] gardener.

bāghīcha [باغیچه] a small garden in which flowers, fruits, or vegetables are grown.

bahā [بها] splendor, beauty, glory.

bahāna [بهانه] excuse, pretext.

bāhith-i jadīd [باحثِ جدید] modern searcher, seeker.

Bahlūl [بهلول] epithet of Wahab ibn ʿAmr, a historical figure who feigned madness to speak truth to power.

Bahrayn [بحرین] (historical region of) Bahrain.

bahr-i āh [بحر آه] sea of lament.

bahr-i ranj [بحر رنج] sea of affliction.

ba-kār [بکار] useful.

bakht [بخت] luck.

bālīn [بالین] bed(ding).

bālisht [بالشت] pillow, cushion.

banda [بنده] servant (of God), slave; human being; a humble way to say "I, me."

bāng [بانگ] sound, noise.

bāng-i nay [بانگ نی] sound of the reed flute.

barbād [برباد] ruined, wasted, gone with the wind.

bardāsht [برداشت] bear, tolerate.

barsāt [برسات] the rainy, monsoon season of the Indian Subcontinent.

bas [بَس] enough.

bashar [بَشر] human (being), mankind.

basīt [بسيط] simple (person or thing), simpleton.

bāzār [بازار] (open air) market, bazaar.

bāzār-parast [بازار پرست] market-worshipping.

bazm [بَزْم] party, assembly, feast.

bēhikmat [بینحکمت] lacking wisdom.

bēkār [بینکار] idle, good-for-nothing, useless, helpless.

bēkas [بینکس] lacking a companion, lonely, friendless.

bēnām [بیننام] nameless, anonymous.

bēwafā [بینوفا] treacherous, faithless.

bēwatan [بینوطن] without country, foreigner.

bēzār [بیزار] weary of, apathetic.

bismil, go to [تو گوِ بسمل] to be slaughtered, to die (hyperbolic).

bū [بو] fragrance, smell.

burda [بُرده] cloak, mantle.

but-parastī [بُتپرستی] idol-worship, paganism.

buzdil [بُزدِل] goat-hearted, i.e. a coward.

chāy [چای] tea.

chī guftī? [چي گُفتي؟] P. what did you say?

dahr [دهر] eon, long period of time; fate.

dām [دام] trap, net, snare; price.

dam [دم] breath; moment, instant; blood.

dam'a [دمعه] tear (from eye).

dance bismil [دَنس بِسمل] dance like an animal being slaughtered, i.e. dance in a frenzy.

dard-i ishtiyāq [درد اشتیاق] pain of longing.

darkār [درکار] necessary.

darmān [درمان] remedy, cure.

dast dar dast [دست در دست] hand in hand, holding hands.

dāstān [دستان] fable, romance, tale.

dastūr [دستور] permission, law, canon.

dēws [دیو] dev, a demon from Persian mythology.

dhāt [ذات] self, essence.

dīda [دیده] eye, vision, sight.

dīdār [دیدار] visitation, seeing the belovèd.

dil [دِل] heart.

dilbāz [دِلباز] lover who plays with hearts.

dil-i shikasta [دِل شِكسته] broken heart.

dilrubā [دِلربا] stealer of hearts.

dilshikastagī [دلشكستگي] heartbreak.

dirakht-naward [دِرختنَورد] tree-climber.

dōst [دوست] friend.

dōstān [دوستان] friends.

du [دو] two.

du'ā [دُعا] prayer, supplication.

dunyā [دنيا] (lower, material) world.

dūr [دور] far.

duzd [دُزد] thief.

fajr [فجر] dawn.

fāl [فال] lot, omen, augury.

fanā [فنا] spiritual annihilation, annihilation of the self.

fardā [فردا] tomorrow, future.

farhang [فرهنگ] culture.

farq [فرق] difference, distinction.

fāsh [فاش] exposed, revealed.

fāsid [فاسد] corrupt, putrefied.

fatwā [فتوى] (religion) legal opinion.

firāq [فراق] separation.

firāsh [فراش] mattress, couch, bedding.

fitrat [فِطرت] innate human nature.

fuhsh [فُحش] insult, abuse; obscene acts.

fulān [فُلان] so-and-so person, stranger.

fulk [فُلك] (Noah's) ark.

gadā [گدا] beggar; spiritual seeker.

garēbān [گرِبان] collar.

gēsū [گِيسو] curl, lock, ringlet.

ghāfil [غافل] thoughtless, inattentive.

gham [غم] grief, sorrow, chagrin.

ghayr [غير] another person; rival, enemy.

ghūl [غول] ghoul, a monster from Arabian mythology.

ghussa [غصه] grief; anger.

gird-i sarā [گرد سرا] at the periphery of your abode.

giryān [گريان] crying, weeping.

gōsht-khōrī [گوت خوزي] eating another's flesh, i.e. backbiting, slandering.

gul [گل] flower(s).

gumrāhī [گُمراهي] state of being lost, of having lost one's way.

hāl [حال] state, status, situation, condition, health.

hāl-i zār [حال زار] aggrieved condition.

halqa [حقله] a circle of mystics or suchlike.

hama-dān [همه دان] all-knower, omniscient.

ham-fikrān [همفکران] plur. of *ham-fikr* [همفکر] like-minded, one who thinks similarly.

hāmiz [حامض] sour, acidic.

Haqq [حق] God.

haqq [حق] truth; fact; right (legal, religious, etc.)

har [هر] each, every.

hargiz [هرگز] never.

hawā [هوا] air, wind, weather, breeze.

hawā [هوى] desire, passion; longing, attachment.

hāy [هاي] oh, woe is me!

hayā [حيا] diffidence, modesty.

hayādārān [حياداران] plur. of *hayādār* [حيادار], modest, shy.

hayāt-angēz [حيات انگيز] life-giving.

hayf ay hayf [حيف اي حيف] what a pity!

hayrān [حيران] surprised, confused.

hāzirīn [حاضرين] attendees, audience.

hikāyat [حكايت] story.

hirqat [حرقت] burn.

hudhud [هُدهُد] hoopoe.

husbān [حُسبان] consideration, thought.

huzn-u-ghamzada [حُزن و غَم زده] struck, afflicted by sadness and melancholy.

Īd-i Ramazān [عيد رمضان] Eid al-Fitr, the Islamic festival marking the end of Ramadan.

imrōz [امروز] today.

imtihān [امتحان] test.

insān [انسان] human (being), man.

ishq [عِشق] (divine; extreme, all-consuming) love, passion.

ishq-bāwar [عشقباور] a believer in divine love, passion.

ishqam! amān! kafā! [عشقم! أمان! كفى!] my love! mercy! enough!

ishtiyāq [اشتياق] longing.

Iskandar [اسكندر] Alexander the Macedonian.

istikān(a) [استكان، استكانه] small glass used for tea.

itāb [عتاب] reproach.

itr [عِطْر] fragrance.

jadīd [جديد] new, modern.

jādūgar [جادوگر] sorcerer, sorceress.

jafā [جفا] emotional cruelty or coldness.

jahān [جهان] world.

jām [جام] cup, glass.

jamāl [جمال] beauty.

jām-i jam [جام جام] a mythical cup used by ancient Persian kings to see the future.

jān [جان] soul, life-force, energy.

jangal [جنگل] jungle.

jān-i jān [جان جان] soul of my soul, a term of endearment.

Jasha'-ville [جشعفل] "Gluttonville", a very real town.

jild [جلد] volume, tome, bound book.

jōsh [جوش] boil, ardor, excitement.

jubba [جبه] an outer robe, with full sleeves and long skirts, and open in front.

kabāb [کباب] meat in pieces and roasted on skewers.

kadar [کدر] sadness, sorrow, anxiety.

kahkashān [کهکشان] galaxy, milky way.

kākul [کاکل] lock, ringlet, curl.

kalī [کلی] (Urdu) blossom, bud.

kalimāt [کلامات] words, plur. of *kalima* [کلمه].

kambakht [کمبخت] unlucky, unfortunate.

kāmilān [کاملان] plur. of *kāmil* [کامل] spiritually perfect.

kanz [کنز] treasure.

kār [کار] work, deed, task, effort; *have no kār* to pay no heed to.

karak [کرك] a type of spiced, milk tea, from the Urdu کڑک (*kaṛak* "bolt of thunder",), lit. 'thundery tea.'

karambakhshī [کرمبخشي] granting a favor or kindness.

kāsh ke [کاش که] I wish, would that.

kashmīr [کشمیر] cashmere, an expensive type of cloth.

kayfi [کَیفي] reveler, merrymaker.

khāk [خاك] soil, dust.

khalq [خلق] people, society, masses; created beings, creatura.

khamīda [خمیده] bent.

kharāb [خراب] (n. adj.) ruin, wreck, (place of) desolation; bad, broken, destroyed.

khār-u-khūn [خار و خون] thorns and blood.

khār-u-nār [خار و نار] thorns and fire.

khātir [خاطر] cogitation, remembrance.

khatt [خط] letter.

khawf-i Khudā [خوف خدا] fear of God.

khayt-i zarīn [خیط زرین] golden thread.

Khudā [خدا] God, Lord; lord.

Khudāwand [خداوند] God, Lord; lord.

Khudā-yi Sūq [خدای سوق] God of the Market.

khud-parast [خودپرست] self-worshipping.

khuluq-i zāhidān [خُلق زاهدان] ethics, behavior of the ascetics.

Khurāsān [خراسان] a historical region of Central Asia and Iran.

khushbū [خوشبو] n.adj. fragrant, sweet smelling; fragrance.

khushhālān [خوشحالان] plur. of *khushhāl* [خوشحال] happy people.

khutba [خطبه] sermon.

khwābīda [خوابیده] sleeping, slumbering.

khwāja [خواجه] master, owner, man of distinction.

kinz [کنز] treasure.

kōshish [کوشش] effort, undertaking.

kū [کو] alleyway, street.

kūcha [کوچه] alley, lane.

kunj-u-sū [کنج و سو] corner and direction.

kūza [کوزه] a type of earthenware.

laban [لبن] a type of dairy drink based on yoghurt, popular in the Arab World.

lāla-rukhsār [لاله رخسار] tulip-cheeked.

Lāmakān [لامکان] "no-place," a divine realm beyond physicality.

lāsh [لاش] corpse, dead body.

lawh [لوح] tablet of (destiny).

lisān [لسان] tongue; language.

Luqmān [لقمان] a wise man mentioned in the Qur'an.

lutf [لطف] kindness, favor.

lutf-i āsh*(ë)nā* [لطف آشنا] kindness for the belovèd.

lutf-u-karam [لطف و کرم] kindness and favor.

mabhūt [مبهوت] shocked, surprised.

magar [مگر] but, however; only.

Maghrib [مغرب] the Arabic/Islamic West.

maghrūr [مغرور] proud, vain.

mahabhat-sitēz [محبت ستیز] love-hating, hostile to love.

mahfil [محفل] (place of) assembly, congregation, venue (where poetry is performed).

majlis [مجلس] assembly, congregation, meeting place.

majnūn [مجنون] crazy, insane, Jinn-possessed.

makhmūr [مخمور] (spiritually) intoxicated.

malākāna [مَلاکانه] angelic.

malāmat [ملامت] reproach.

mālik [مالک] land-owner, landlord.

mantiq [منطق] reasoning, logic. A reference to Attār's Mantiq at-Tayr, *Conference of the Birds.*

manzil [مَنزِل] abode, stage.

manzūr [منظور] seen, visible.

maqbūr [مقبور] dead, entombed.

mār [مار] snake, serpent.

ma'rafat-jūyān [معرفتجویان] seekers of knowledge.

mardum [مَردُم] people.

markab [مرکب] ship, vessel, vehicle.

masht-i khāk [مشت خاک] fistful of dirt

masjid [مسجد] mosque.

masmūm [مسموم] poisoned.

mast [مَست] (spiritually) intoxicated, drunk.

may [می] wine.

maykada [مَیکده] tavern, pub, wine cellar.

miskīn [مِسکین] poor, pauper; wretched, afflicted.

miskīn-i mubtalā [مسکین مُبتلی] afflicted wretch.

mu'min [مؤمن] believer, faithful.

mudām [مُدام] wine.

mudān [مُدان] one condemned.

muftī [مُفتی] Muslim legal expert.

muhājir [مهاجر] migrant.

mul [مُل] wine.

murgh [مُرغ] bird; chicken.

murīd [مُرید] disciple, student.

murshid [مُرشد] guide.

mushkil [مُشکل] difficult, problematic.

mūsīqī [موسیقی] (traditional) music.

muzd [مُزد] wages.

nādān [نادان] foolish, simple, ignorant.

nafas [نَفَس] breath; soul, life.

nafs [نَفْس] spirit, soul.

nahīf [نحیف] (of people), very thin.

nahr [نهر] river.

na-insān [نا انسان] non-human.

nākhudā [ناخُدا] sea-captain, skipper.

nāl [نال] v.n. lament, complain(t).

nāl ū āh [نال و آه] lament and ah.

nāla [ناله] lament, complaint.

nālān [نالان] (one who is) lamenting.

nālīda [نالیده] lamenting, weeping.

namāz [نماز] (Islamic) prayer, worship.

nān [نان] bread, food.

nāqisān [ناقصان] plur. of *nāqis* [ناقص] incomplete, imperfect; spiritually deficient.

nār [نار] (hell) fire.

nawwāb [نوّاب] ruler, governor, lord.

nay [نی] (reed) flute.

nayzan [نَیزَن] piper, flautist.

nāz [ناز] coquetry.

nazar [نظر] eyesight, (field of) vision; appearance; opinion.

nāzuk-salīqa [نازُك سلیقه] soft-natured.

nigāh [نگاه] sight, look, glance, attention.

nīyat [نیّت] intention.

nūr [نور] light.

nūr-i nahār [نور نهار] light of day.

pādshāh [پادهشاه] king, emperor, sovereign.

parī [پری] fairy, fay, nymph.

parī-paykar [پری پَیکر] possessing

a fairy-like form.

parīrukh [پريرخ] angel-faced, fairy-faced.

payghāmbar [پيغامبر] messenger, prophet.

pēchīda [پيچيده] complicated, twisted.

phūl [پهول] (Urdu) flower(s).

pīr [پير] old man; religious guide or master, a saint.

qabā [قبا] (Turkic) coarse, vulgar.

qadd [قدّ] height, stature, poise.

qahwa [قَهْوه] coffee; historically, mulled wine.

qalandar [قلندر] a Sufi itinerant who resounces the material aspects of life.

qalb [قلب] heart, core, inner life.

qand [قَند] rock sugar, rock candy.

qasā'id [قصائد] plur. of *qasīda* [قصيده] long-form poem.

qasam [قَسَم] oath, vow.

qaws [قَوس] rainbow.

qazā [قضا] fate, predestination.

qirmiz [قِرمِز] crismon (color).

qisas [قِصص] plur. of *qissa* [قِصّه] story.

qiyāmat [قيامت] Day of Resurrection and Judgment.

qubba [قُبه] (mosque) dome.

qurbān(ī) [قُربانِي] sacrifice.

ra'y-i khalq [رأي خلق] people's opinion.

raftār [رفتار] behavior, manner; way.

rag [رگ] vein.

rāh [راه] way, path; manner.

rahmat-i āshënā [رحمت آشنا] mercy for the belovèd.

rang [رنگ] color; type, sort.

ranj [رنج] suffering, affliction.

ranjīda [رنجيده] grieved, afflicted.

raqīb [رقيب] adversary, enemy.

rashk-i qamar [رشك قمر] envy of the moon, i.e. beautiful belovèd.

rasm [رَسم] custom, tradition; drawing.

rawān [روان] soul, spirit, psyche.

rāz [راز] secret, mystery.

rind [رِند] a dedicated Sufi who affects moral debauchery.

rū [رو] face, countenance; surface.

rū bar qafā [رو بر قفا] head turned backward.

rūh [روح] spirit, soul.

rukh [رُخ] cheek; face.

rummān [رُمان] pomegranate.

ruswā [رُسوا] disgraced, ignominious.

sabr [صبر] patience.

sāda [ساده] simple, naïve.

safā [صفا] peace of mind, tranquility.

sāfī [صافي] pure; tranquil.

sāhir [ساحر] charming,

enchanting.
sāhir-u-muskir [ساحر و مُسکر]
enchanting and intoxicating.
sakht [سخت] hard; *sar-sakht*
[سرسخت] "hard-headed," i.e.
obstinate.
salāmat [سلامت] safety.
sanjīda [سنجیده] serious, grave.
sāqī [ساقی] cup-bearer.
sar [سر] head.
sarā [سرا] abode, house, palace.
sarāy [سرای] abode, house,
palace.
sarsakhtī [سرسختی] obstinacy,
stubbornness, lit. "head-
hardness."
sarw-qadd [سروقد] cypress-
statured.
sēr [سیر] satiated, satisfied, not
hungry.
shā'ir [شاعر] poet.
shāhāna [شاهانه] royal, kingly.
shāh-i husn [شاه حسن] king of
beauty.
shakar [شکر] sugar.
shām [شام] eve(ning).
sham'a-yi mahfil [شمعه محفل]
candle of the assembly or
congregation.
shān [شان] glory, authority,
power.
shāndār [شاندار] grand, splendid;
a person of high rank or quality.
sharāb [شراب] wine.

sharm [شرم] shame, modesty.
shātir [شاطر] clever, sly; thief,
conman.
shawq [شوق] longing, yearning.
shaydā [شیدا] maddened by love.
shaykhī [شیخی] my teacher, my
guide.
shi'r-i fardā [شعر فردا] poetry of
tomorrow, i.e. the future.
shifā [شفا] cure, recovery.
shikāyat [شکایت] complaint.
shirīn [شرین] sweet.
sīdī [سیدی] my lord, mister.
sirr [سرّ] secret, mystery.
siyah-post [سیه پوست] dark-
skinned.
sū [سو] direction, side.
sūq [سوق] market, marketplace.
ta'ākul [تأکل] erosion, being eaten
away.
ta'rīf [تعریف] (offer a)
compliment.
tabīb [طبیب] physician, doctor.
tāli' [طالع] luck, lot, fortune, star;
what or who arises.
tamāshā [تماشا] spectacle, show.
tambal [تمبل] lazy, indolent,
good-for-nothing.
tan [تن] body, person
tang [تنگ] tight, constrained;
dil-tangī [دلتنگی] lit. "heart-
tightness," yearning, longing,
homesickness.
tanhā [تنها] lonely, lone, only.

tanz [طنز] banter, ridicule, sartire, mockery.

tāq [طاق] a small cove in a wall for storing things.

tarab [طرب] enjoyment (of music).

tarkīda [ترکیده] abandoned.

thaqāfat [ثقافت] culture.

tīr [تیر] arrow.

tishna [تشنه] (spiritually) thirsty, seeking.

tukhm-i shakk [تخم شكّ] seed of doubt.

u [و] (connection particles, especially in compounds) and.

uff [أف] uff, an exclamation of exasperation or frustration.

Umān [عُمان] Oman.

umīd, umēd [أمید، أميد] hope.

umm [أم] mother.

umr [عُمر] (duration of) life.

wālī [والي] governor, prefect.

wasl [وَصل] union with the belovèd.

wāy [واي] woe!

wayrān [وَیران] devastated, desolate.

wayrānī [وَیرانی] devastation (psychological, material), desolation.

waznbāz [وُزنباز] a person who uses dishonest scales, lit. "weight-cheater."

wirth(a) [ورثه] inheritance, heritage.

wisāl [وصال] union with the belovèd.

yād-khandīda [یادخندیده] smiling at memories.

Yaman [یَمَن] Yemen.

yār [یار] lover, friend, companion.

Yūsuf [یوسُف] the prophet Joseph.

zabān [زبان] tongue; language.

zāhid [زاهد] devout, ascetic, hermit.

zāhir [ظاهر] exterior, outer material aspect.

ẓālimī ʿafā [ظالمي عفا] my tyrant/ oppressor has forgiven (me).

zamāna [زمانه] epoch, era, Zeitgeist, world.

zamīr [ضمیر] conscience.

zammār [زمار] piper.

zanjīr [زنجیر] chain.

zann [ظن] conjecture, suspicion.

zarb-i daff [ضرب دفّ] playing or beating the *daff* (frame drum).

zardōzī [زردوزَي] gold(en) embroidery.

zindagī [زِندگی] life.

zindān [زندان] prison, jail.

zulf [زُلف] (hair) curl, tress.

zunnār [زنّار] a waist-belt formerly worn by Zoroastrians or Christians.

Acknowledgements

I wish to acknowledge my friend Muhammad Ali Mojaradi for his continuous encouragement and inspiration. I am also grateful to R.K. for being the ultimate source of much knowledge and help regarding form and meter.

⸙

About the Author

Wael Almahdi is a poet, translator, and healthcare professional from Bahrain. He is a recipient of a High Commendation from the Stephen Spender Poetry Translation Prize and his Arabic translations include works by the National Poet of Wales and Lewis Carroll's *Jabberwocky*. He has also translated for the 2024 Diriyah Biennale and Won Buddhism in South Korea. In recent years, he has delved into the rich tradition that blends themes, vocabulary, and spirit from Arabic and Persian—a poetic heritage which has deeply influenced major languages like Urdu and Turkish. This exploration inspired the creation of Mashriqi English, a fresh poetic register that merges the expressive depth of Modern English with the multifaceted, centuries-old Perso-Arabic poetic tradition.

About Crescent Books

Crescent Books is committed to publishing works that challenge the conventional and celebrate the diverse voices that enrich our understanding of faith, culture, and history. As a small, passionate team of book lovers, we guide authors through the publishing process with editorial freedom and genuine partnership. We serve our communities by producing books that inspire, provoke thought, and entertain, creating transformative reading experiences that connect with a broad audience and open doors to new perspectives on our ever-evolving world.

Other Titles by Crescent Books

The Expansion of Islam by Sami Frashëri, 2025

The Book of Great Quotes by Flamur Vehapi, 2025

When My Absence Becomes a Moon by Laureta Rexha, 2024

Grains of Destiny by Brandon Mayfield, 2024

Berke Khan of the Golden Horde by Flamur Vehapi, 2024

The World According to Sami Frashëri by Flamur Vehapi, 2024

The Spectacular Escape by Burhan Al-Din Fili, 2023

Atheism Versus Belief by Brandon Mayfield, 2023

Kosovo: A Brief Chronology by Flamur Vehapi, 2023

Verses of the Heart: Poems by Flamur Vehapi, 2021

Ertugrul Ghazi: A Very Short Biography by Flamur Vehapi, 2021